Eccentric Travellers
John Keay

ECCENTRIC TRAVELLERS

ARIEL BOOKS

BRITISH BROADCASTING CORPORATION

This book was suggested when planning the radio documentary series of the same name. The series was produced by Alan Haydock to whom I owe a great debt of thanks; it has as always been a pleasure to work with him. His colleague, Barry Carman, introduced me to the amazing James Holman, and Simon Nuttall suggested the inclusion of the elusive William Gifford Palgrave. For the radio series the Charles Waterton script was written by J-P. de Rohan. It was J-P's passionate advocacy of Waterton which suggested the whole series and so the book. I thank him profusely.

My thanks also to Canon Hugh Evan Hopkins for letting me see the typescript of his new biography of Joseph Wolff, and Jennifer Fry for finding all the pictures, to Stephen Davies, Toby Roxburgh and John Murray for editorial encouragement, – and to Julia.

Published by the British Broadcasting Corporation
35 Marylebone High Street London WIM 4AA

First published in 1982 by John Murray (Publishers) Ltd and the BBC
First paperback edition 1985
© John Keay 1982

ISBN 0 563 20280 7

Typeset by Phoenix Photosetting, Chatham
Printed and bound in Great Britain by
Mackays of Chatham Ltd, Kent

This book is set in 10 on 11 point Ehrhardt

For my mother

Contents

Introduction

Even the Uzbegs have a word for it. After carefully scrutinising his plump and unwelcome visitor the villainous Amir of Bukhara guffawed, 'thou star with a tail, thou *eccentric* man'. At the time Dr Joseph Wolff did not argue. Content to describe himself as a Christian dervish – and sporting his canonicals to prove it – he had just forced his way into the holiest city in Islamic Central Asia. Later, repeating the story, he seemed rather to relish the idea of being thought eccentric; it was definitely an improvement on 'crazy' or the then equally disparaging 'enthusiastic'.

It was also an improvement on 'quack', 'blackmailer' and 'buffoon'. Captain Philip Thicknesse had been called by so many unpleasant names that he would have taken for a compliment something as mild as 'eccentric'. He, if anyone, positively cultivated eccentricity. He appreciated its entertainment value and he knew that much is forgiven the man who can make people laugh.

But Wolff and Thicknesse are the exceptions. Although I trust the inclusion in this book of the other characters will prove justified, I doubt whether they personally would have welcomed it. Charles Waterton, surely the most bizarre of all, made his feelings very clear. When a fellow naturalist described him as somewhat eccentric he bristled as only the crew-cut can. The accusation he described as like an undeserved pinch and it was duly repaid with a hefty academic punch. To the phenomenal James Holman it would have been more like an unkind jibe; no one tried so valiantly to observe the social conventions as Holman. And as for the three men of genius, Thomas Manning, Gifford Palgrave and Gottlieb Leitner, they surely would have ignored any such foolish insinuation. To them eccentricity was no more than the trumped-up consolation of a meagre intellect contemplating something beyond its comprehension.

Certainly eccentricity lies mainly in the eye of the beholder. These seven characters represent a personal choice and, though by definition each is unique, I hope that certain shared characteristics may reconcile them to inclusion. In the first place they are all men of uncommon stature. Eccentric behaviour is not the result of ignoring logic but of pursuing it to unusual extremes. Such excessive single-mindedness, far from being a handicap, can be highly efficacious. Thomas Manning was the first Englishman to reach the Tibetan capital of Lhasa, Gifford Palgrave the first to enter the Arabian capital of Riyadh, and Gottlieb Leitner the first to write an account of Gilgit in the high Hindu Kush. 'What is Gilgit?' it was asked; had Leitner invented it? He had surely invented the peculiar Dards who lived there and about whom he claimed to be the greatest, indeed the only, authority. Palgrave, too, was accused of fanciful descriptions of the Arabs, and Manning of the Chinese. Both supposedly fabricated itineraries. Yet nowadays Palgrave is acknowledged as one of the greatest Arabists, and Manning as an outstanding Sinologist. Even Leitner emerges as a linguist and ethnologist some fifty years ahead of his time.

No one believed Waterton either. He described the South American ant-eater as never walking on the soles of its feet and the sloth as never walking on its feet at all. To naturalists of the day this was preposterous – as preposterous as riding on an alligator or wrestling with a boa-constrictor. But they should have known better than to differ with the only man who had tried these feats. Waterton is now revered as an outstanding field naturalist for the pre-Darwin days and a pioneer in conservation.

Nor are scientific and academic achievements the only claims to celebrity. There were other ways for a traveller to make a name for himself. Wolff was wont to regret his inability to read either map or compass; so, for different reasons, was Holman; Thicknesse appears never to have heard of such things. Yet in their day these three enjoyed considerable reputations. Wolff's various crusades so captured the popular imagination that he became a household name; what he lacked in wit and wisdom he more than compensated for by his irresistible faith. For the terrible Thicknesse it was more a question of notoriety than fame; he scandalised two whole generations. Yet in his travels the Captain was revealed in an altogether more favourable light. Those who normally regarded him as an unspeakable horror suddenly realised that beneath the impossible exterior lurked originality, humour and much candour.

Holman was, quite simply, 'the greatest traveller of all time'. His affliction may have contributed to his fame and may subsequently have accounted for his being ignored. But that is beside the point. The interesting thing is, had he not been totally blind, he would never have felt the need to embark on his improbable journeys. As with Thicknesse, travel was a matter of justifying his existence. It was worth going to extremes.

The same could of course be said of many other travellers and explorers. Eccentricity and travel were both forms of escape from the conventions of a rigid society. The combination of the two was so common that the eccentric traveller became as much a stock figure as the eccentric academic or the eccentric aristocrat. There must be dozens who qualify. What of the complex and brooding Richard Burton who was forever disappearing into the murky depths of oriental society? Or Ludwig Leichardt whose strange affair with the Australian Outback provided the inspiration for Patrick White's impossible *Voss*? Or Lady Hester Stanhope, the niece of William Pitt who presided over her own Levantine court and managed to outrage even Joseph Wolff? These, and many more, were eccentrics whose fame ranks with the greatest.

But they are not in these pages. Partly this is due to space, partly because they are already well known, and partly because they are distinctly less endearing. Eccentricity of too deep and tortured a hue is no pleasure to contemplate. It needs recognisably human tints. True, seven characters with nothing more than devastating incompetence to recommend them would become tedious fare. But so too is the grim professionalism of men like Burton. How much more lovable is a bungling genius like Manning or a frightful busybody like Thicknesse. And how fortunate that celebrity and distinction never inhibited Waterton's love of pranks or Wolff's messianic explosions.

At odds with society, the eccentric traveller typically approached his foreign field with a more open mind than his straight-laced colleagues. Not only were his particular idiosyncrasies endearing but so was his usually sympathetic attitude towards native society. Leitner was as concerned for the protection and conservation of his Dards as Waterton was for his fauna. Manning came to revere both the Chinese and the Tibetans, Palgrave nearly abandoned his heart and his vocation to the Arabs, and Wolff found goodness bordering on sanctity in Mohammedan, Christian, Jew and Brahmin. Even Thicknesse, who enjoyed, in Edith Sitwell's words, 'that peculiar and satisfactory knowledge of infallibility which is the hallmark and birthright of the English nation', was no exception. He rushed to the defence of the then universally unpopular French, he had a good word to say for the Negro slaves, and he was one of the foremost apologists for the American Indians. Such sentiments were not then calculated to win many admirers. Today they, and the delightful characters who proclaimed them, deserve better of us.

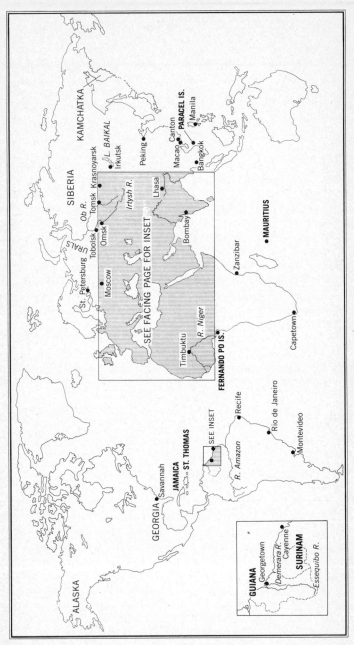

ALASKA

GEORGIA

Savannah

JAMAICA

ST. THOMAS

SEE INSET

R. Amazon

Recife

Rio de Janeiro

Montevideo

GUIANA

Georgetown

Demerara R.

Cayenne

SURINAM

Essequibo R.

KAMCHATKA

PARACEL IS.

Manila

Canton

L. BAIKAL

Krasnoyarsk

Peking

Macao

Bangkok

Irkutsk

SIBERIA

Tomsk

Ob R.

Irtysh R.

Lhasa

Tobolsk

Omsk

Bombay

URALS

St. Petersburg

Moscow

SEE FACING PAGE FOR INSET

Zanzibar

MAURITIUS

R. Niger

Timbuktu

FERNANDO PO IS.

Capetown

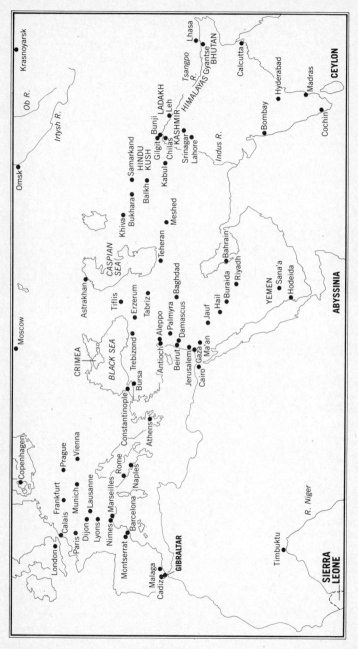

I
'A Free Citizen'
Captain Philip Thicknesse

The Grand Tour of two hundred years ago was not everybody's idea of fun. For every aristocratic English mind improved by the experience of continental *savoir faire* there was a cherished reputation ruined by a pouting temptress and a family fortune lost at rouge-et-noir. That indulgence which would later be shown to the tweedy English tourist with his box camera and his atrocious French was not lavished on the bewigged dandy who preceded him. The young and spirited eighteenth-century Englishman was fair game. Newly rich, arrogant, Protestant, and unloved, he was pursued unmercifully and flattered only to be fleeced. He was also exposed to more traditional dangers. Compared to home, the roads were more dangerous, the cities more dirty, and disease more prevalent. And before he could savour any of them he had to brave the horrors of a channel crossing.

Between Dover and Calais a host of small craft vied for business. All were cramped, uncomfortable and at the mercy of the wind. If you travelled with your vehicle you needed a whole boat to yourself. The carriage would be lashed to the vessel and the passengers either lashed to their seats or squeezed into a small cabin. Outside the frantic horses kicked and the waves slurped over the gunwales. The voyage could last days rather than hours.

At Calais, the tide being favourable and the skipper accommodating, you might get into the harbour. Equally you might be transhipped outside it or simply beached on the coast – horses, carriage and occupants then being faced with an undignified dash through the breakers and a hard slog across the dunes. The immediate consolation was the prospect of recuperating at Monsieur Dessein's excellent Hôtel d'Angleterre and catching up on the latest expatriate gossip. Calais – and Boulogne whence the stage plied to Paris – boasted a lively and ever-changing society. Between London and Versailles, Bath and Baden-Baden, the famous and the fashionable drifted to and fro. So too did the infamous – adventurers and outcasts, fugitives from British society and justice.

Captain Philip Thicknesse, landing at Calais in 1775, would like to have considered himself as one of the illustrious. His enemies, who were many, firmly classed him with the refugee criminals. And even he admitted to being on the run. But he was also a genuine and inquisitive tourist travelling for amusement or, as he put it, 'to see what is to be seen'. Unlike most of his contemporaries he was deeply fond of France. Ten years previously Tobias Smollett had travelled south to Italy and written a tirade against French manners and customs. Thicknesse took strong exception to Smollett's account and was determined to set the record straight. It was true that for the indiscreet youth there were perils of every possible description; but for one in the afternoon of life there were only minor irritations. French inn-keepers, for instance, tended to be blackguards, the laundry-maids invariably trimmed off the lace of one's handkerchiefs to make borders for their night-caps, and every *monsieur*, regardless of class or age, made it a point of honour to attempt the seduction of one's wife. But on the credit side the cuisine was superb, the wine was cheap, the upper classes were the most civilised and hospitable in the world, and though wives were at risk virgins were rarely molested.

To prove this last point the Captain was travelling with his two teenage daughters. Mrs Thicknesse was also present – presumably he did not consider her susceptible to Gallic charms. It was truly, therefore, a family holiday and like many such a jaunt had to be conducted on what he called 'the frugal plan'. This necessitated an immediate change of vehicle. For twenty-two guineas he sold his four-wheel postchaise and horses to the proprietor of the Hôtel d'Angleterre, buying, for half the price, a two-wheel cabriolet and a handsome horse 'a little touched in the wind' perhaps but soon a firm favourite and named, inevitably, 'Callee'. It was rather like exchanging the family saloon for a modest little convertible. With undisguised pride Thicknesse fitted out his new acquisition 'with every convenience I could contrive'. Callee entered the shafts, the ladies were stowed in a sofa-like seat under the awning, and wearing his uniform of a Captain in Colonel Jefferies' Marines, Thicknesse mounted the box, took the reins, and headed south for Spain and the sunshine.

It was June, the corn was already high and so too near St Omer was a fine crop of tobacco. This reminded the Captain of his early travels in America. Lost in reverie he took a wrong turning, was directed across the fields rather than turn back ('a circumstance I much hate') and stumbled upon a village whose inhabitants 'had never before seen an Englishman!'

'We found one of these villagers as ready to boil our tea-kettle, provide butter, milk etc. as we were for our breakfasts. And during the preparation of it, I believe every man, woman and child of the hamlet was come down to look at us. . . . There was such general delight in the faces of every age and so much civility shown to us that I caught a temporary cheerfulness in this village which I had not felt for some months before, and which I intend to carry with me. I therefore took out my guitar and played till I set the whole assembly in motion. And some, in spite of their wooden shoes, and others without any, danced in a manner not to be seen amongst our English peasants.'

One must assume that as to personal effects the Thicknesse family was travelling light. The cabriolet did boast a capacious trunk, forerunner of the car boot; but this was reserved for Callee's big drinking bowl – and for the musical instruments. As Miss Ann Ford, Mrs Thicknesse had once been a notable songstress. Accompanying herself on the viol da gamba, the guitar and the musical glasses, she had caused a sensation; not all of it was due to the fact that her performance invariably concluded with arrest by her irate father.

For travelling purposes the viol da gamba, a cello-like instrument, had had to be left behind. But there were still the Captain's guitar and fiddle, Mrs Thicknesse's base viol and guitar, and 'other musical instruments' which must surely mean the musical glasses. Faced with these unlikely effects, a Spanish customs officer would – and did – conclude that he was dealing with a party of strolling players.

Not surprising then that the peasants of Normandy turned out in force when the strumming Thicknesses stopped for breakfast. But long before the dancing began, their attention would have been arrested by another peculiarity of the Thicknesse ménage. Besides the beribboned womenfolk and excluding the faithful Callee, the cabriolet had three other occupants. One, the Captain's spaniel, as often as not trotted alongside. Mrs Thicknesse's pet parakeet was also free to fly, or ride, wherever it pleased. But for some reason, which the Captain could only explain by crediting the bird with the soul of one of his wife's departed lovers, it preferred to sit on its mistress's bosom or occasionally hang by the beak from her tippet. The Captain, a jealous man at the best of times, had no love for the parakeet; but in Jocko, his pet monkey and indisputably the star of the show, he found a willing subject in which to sublimate his own unusual personality. Jocko liked to ride postilion and, Callee having no objections, he did so. The opportunity was too good to miss; a special livery was commissioned. In red jacket laced with silver, jack-boots, a hard hat, and a detachable pigtail, the monkey, crop in hand, bestrode his mount and proudly conducted the party. Whole towns would be brought to a standstill by this unusual sight and it was only in the interests of public order that Jocko could be persuaded to dismount.

What struck Thicknesse most forcibly was that the French, unlike the English, never ridiculed him. Their curiosity about Jocko was excessive and their delight unbounded, but there was no hint of a sneer. It was true even of the simple villagers near St Omer. They were the poorest of the poor and their shoes were 'like sauce-boats'. But they resented not the intrusion of travellers and they made no attempt to profit by it. 'I could moralise here a little,' wrote the Captain, and did just that. 'The behaviour of the inhabitants of this little village had a very forcible effect on me because it brought me back to my earlier days and reminded me of the reception I met with in America by what we now call the *savage* Indians.' It was all of thirty-five years since he had last crossed the Atlantic. But as he once again took to the road the memory of those distant days came flooding back.

Born in 1719 the son of a Northampton rector he had been educated locally and then as a gratis scholar at Westminster. The school was a good one but the young Thicknesse's stay was brief. To relieve his chronic shortage of pocket money he permitted a fellow pupil – and the heir to an earldom – to chastise him with a yard and a half of doubled wax candle at so much a stroke. 'I believe,' he would write in old age, 'I could at this day show upon the backs of my hands the favours frequently conferred upon them by that truly beautiful nobleman.' Nor did he fare much better with the masters. His father had died when he was six; the family had fallen on hard times, and the masters were therefore deprived of those little perquisites which were then considered a necessary token of parental concern. They responded by treating the wretched Thicknesse as a child of no consequence. Frightened and miserable he eventually absconded and – 'a joyful sentence' – was expelled.

His mother forgave him and apprenticed him to a London apothecary. As Thicknesse would later explain, he had gained a little Latin, he was the seventh son 'without a daughter in between', and he had indeed 'stroked away several wens and other disorders such as are apt to disappear without medicine'. What more natural than that he should join the medical profession? Medicine would remain a life-long hobby. Like many an eighteenth-century gentleman Thicknesse never hesitated to pronounce on the bodily functions; he relished the medical controversies of the day and he soon became convinced that most patent medicines were no more than placebos. To the apothecary this represented a dangerous heresy which threatened his livelihood. Thicknesse agreed, relinquished his apprenticeship, and in 1735, aged sixteen, he emigrated to America.

His imagination had been fired by advertisements for the latest and last of the American colonies which had just been founded on a section of coast called Georgia. Here was a chance to begin again under the most encouraging circumstances. For Georgia was not just another colony but a unique experiment. Instead of recruiting settlers indiscriminately, the promoters were looking for men of integrity whose only misfortune was, through no fault of their own, to have been dispossessed (like the one hundred and thirty Highlanders from Inverness who sailed out with him) or financially distressed. Thicknesse thought he fitted this latter category perfectly. He was delighted by the prospect of a society in which insolvency would be no stigma and he was genuinely fired by the altruism of the founders. If anything, he expected rather too much:

'Upon our arrival at Georgia I was much surprised to find the town of Savannah – or rather the spot where the town now stands – situated upon a high bluff of barren land and directly opposite to a low swampy island on the muddy shores of which (within a small compass) I could count at least twenty alligators basking thereon.'

The colony was still struggling to establish itself yet the promoters seemed mainly concerned for its spiritual welfare. To rally the faithful and to convert the natives they had sent out two brothers, fresh from Oxford and fired with an unusual zeal. Their names were John and Charles Wesley and in spite of their subsequent celebrity they were not a success in Savannah. Like the other settlers, Thicknesse took exception to their overbearing behaviour. He resented being counted amongst the elect and, after a speedy fall from grace, he resented being excluded from the elect. He had nothing against Methodism as such, just its methods. The Wesley brothers, so outwardly righteous, were concentrating their efforts on the colony's few young ladies and monopolising their attentions. First there was a row over some compromising letters written by John Wesley to a Miss Sophie Hopkins. Then Charles

Wesley, supposedly intent on saving 'a fair but *frail* lady', managed to goad her into a physical assault on his person. According to Thicknesse, 'she laid violent hands upon him, threw him upon the bed, and threatened him with immediate loss of life – or what some men might deem as dear as life; nor did she dismiss him until she had deprived him of all the Adonis locks which at that time adorned one side of his meek and godly countenance.'

Thicknesse relished such scandals. He spread the news abroad and in time would acquire great notoriety for his character demolitions. 'Dr Viper' he would be called, the man with the venomous tongue and the poisoned pen. But it is worth remembering that there was usually some substance to his slanders. The Wesleys, for instance, did acquire a highly ambiguous reputation in Georgia; some of these stories – and there were many more – can certainly be substantiated. And if the zealous brothers seem a target unworthy of such gossip, one must allow for the fact that already Thicknesse was on the side of the Indians.

His official position in Georgia is not known. He was presumably drawing a small salary perhaps as a clerk or as an ensign in the militia. Soon after his arrival he was sent on some errand to Yamacra, the principal encampment of the local Indians. There he found the chieftain and his squaw – or rather 'king' Tomo Chachi and 'queen' Cenauke – just returned from harvesting oysters. They generously asked him to join them and 'I had the honour of partaking with them a *repas* to which they sat down with as good an appetite as ever European princes did to a barrel of Pyefleet'. Subsequent visits convinced him that in spite of appearances – 'rude dress, painted faces, sliced ears, nose bobs and tattooed skins' – the Indians were as honest a people as any in Christendom. Moreover, 'Tomo Chachi, the Creek Indian king, was not only a very humane man but, I might add, he was a very well-bred man.'

The king had surrendered the site of Savannah, previously his own capital, without demur. He had pleaded for clemency on behalf of a settler who was being birched for molesting an Indian squaw. And, most surprising of all, he had submitted to a visit to London where, suitably painted and feathered, he and Queen Cenauke had been driven to Kensington Palace to pledge their friendship to George II and Queen Caroline.

Happily, from this brief brush with civilisation, the king and his subjects had emerged unscathed. The real danger lay with the colonists. 'Under the name of civilised Christians,' noted Thicknesse, 'they deprive the Indians of their native rights and, what I fear is much worse, of their simplicity of manners and their frugal mode of life . . . instead of which they have got diseases before unknown to them, spiritous liquors which render them frantic, and they are still strangers to everything which belongs to Christianity.'

Even an acid-loaded pen could hardly do justice to such inhumanity. Long before it was remotely fashionable Thicknesse not only espoused the Indian cause but the Indian way of life. He learnt something of their language, he studied their hunting methods and their diet, and he finally set up home on an island up the Savannah river. From the colony he bought only rice 'by way of bread'. The Indians kept him in venison (eaten dipped in honey) and his gun ensured an inexhaustible supply of duck and squirrel (eaten boiled).

'This was the true Robinson Crusoe line of life but it was such as even in those days suited my romantic turn. In this situation I wanted nothing but a female friend and I had almost determined to take to wife one of Queen Cenauke's maids of honour. I seriously paid my addresses to her and she in turn honoured me with the appellation of *Auche* (friend). She received a pair of Indian boots, some paint, a looking glass, a comb and a pair of scissors as tokens of my love.'

All that remained was for the young couple to consummate matters. And, as the lovelorn *auche* graphically put it, 'one buffalo's skin had certainly held us, had not an extraordinary incident arose.' While strolling along the beach of his island playing the flute ('such was the effect of love on an affectionate and warm imagination') he experienced a vision of his mother 'as if she had actually been before me *in propria persona*'.

'My squaw, my island, my Robinson Crusoe plan, instantly lost all their charms. . . . I determined to leave the shadow and seek the substance. I immediately set out for Savannah.'

It was the end of his American adventure. Filial duty, and the misfit's perverse need for the society to which he would never belong, drew him home. He reached England in 1737. He still intended returning to Georgia and he applied for a commission in the new regiment that was being raised for the colony's defence. Strings were pulled in the usual way but something went wrong. Instead of being appointed to Georgia as a Lieutenant he was posted to Jamaica as a Captain. Here there was less scope for one of 'a romantic turn'. The island was being overrun by rats and by escaped slaves. To combat these two menaces a system of bounty payments had been introduced: a bottle of rum for every dozen rat's tails and '£70 for every pair of wild Negro's ears'. The young Captain was despatched inland after the slaves. 'I thank God, however, that in that business I was fortunate for I never gathered a single pair [of ears]. . . . However honourable it may be deemed to invade, disturb or murder men of distant climes, it did not tally with my ideas of justice.'

Looking back he could be justifiably proud of his record of defending under-dogs. The Jamaican slaves never won his heart like the American Indians but he had firmly maintained that they had as much right to the island as the white planters. The same liberal and humane attitude would inform his few dealings with the poor and underprivileged in English society. 'A man of probity and honour' was how one contemporary described him; his 'heart and purse were always open to the unfortunate'.

Another contemporary was less flattering. Thicknesse 'had in a remarkable degree the faculty of lessening the number of his friends and increasing the number of his enemies.' Unfortunately this too was an accurate appraisal. After the interludes in Georgia and Jamaica the Captain's career entered its long and stormy meridian in England. Abroad his benevolence and humanity had distinguished him as the very ideal of the English gentleman. At home, to sustain the same persona amidst a host of nobler and wealthier scions, he resorted to a flamboyance which invited censure and to a sensitivity which imagined still more censure. Only the most fashionable circles attracted him; yet lacking that assurance which comes with family, fortune or fame, the vital balance between dash and decorum ever eluded him.

He married well – indeed he married thrice, his first wife being something of an heiress and his second having a title (both died prematurely and hence his marriage to the musical Miss Ford). His private life was blameless and his finances briefly improved to the extent that he was able to buy a military sinecure – the Governorship of Landguard Fort near Harwich. But the dowries never matched his expectations and his in-laws never welcomed him. He remained a misfit. Eighteenth-century society was lively, thrusting and ruthless. It was sheer force of intellect as much as brilliance which sustained the likes of Dr Johnson. Thicknesse could be just as disagreeable and a good deal more vitriolic, but he lacked the stature of the Doctor. He longed to be the toast of the town but ended up one of society's casualties.

The succession of unsavoury vendettas, libel actions and mock duels which punctuate this period of his life won him only ridicule and, in one case, a spell in prison. Invariably the causes were trivial – one was sparked off by a row over champagne vintages – and the blame as much Thicknesse's as anyone's. They were long, tedious and confusing wrangles which reflect credit on no one. Suffice it to say that his adversaries included fellow officers, medical practitioners and divines. They included the Earl of Coventry, the Lord Chancellor and the Archbishop of Canterbury. They included his two sons and his best friend. They even included the House of Lords: it was a series of letters criticising a judgement in the Lords and published in the press which had eventually precipitated his hurried departure for Calais in 1775. After thirty-five years of back-biting in the salons and courts, it was no wonder that he welcomed the warm-hearted acceptance of the Normandy peasants and detected a cheerfulness which had eluded him for so long. He responded with genial delight. If only the rest of the world were as easy-going and as easily amused.

Punctuating his reminiscences with visits to the odd *cave* and an examination of the crops, the Captain and his ménage reached Rheims just after the coronation there of Louis XVI. This was intentional. 'Having paid two guineas to see the coronation of George III, I determined never more to be put to any extraordinary expense on the score of crowned heads.' Mrs Thicknesse and the girls must have felt hard done by. Instead of a coronation at Rheims they were offered a public execution at Dijon. The Captain understood that the criminal in question fully deserved his punishment and, curious to see how the French managed such matters, he went along. In the event he wished that he had stayed at the inn. The criminal was not simply hung but first *broken*, each limb in turn being smashed with a blunt cleaver. This revolting sight rightly drew forth his indignation, although he conceded that perhaps the lawlessness of the countryside called for a formidable deterrent. Further proofs of the dangers of the highway followed. Near Chalons the cabriolet drew abreast of a line of nine gibbets from which dangled an entire family of bandits – 'a man, his wife, and their seven children who had lived many years by robbery and murder'. Fortunately any sense of unease in the party was quickly dispelled. The ladies greeted the hilly vistas of Burgundy with cries of delight and as they meandered through the vineyards the Captain himself visibly mellowed:

'The prospect from the highest part of the road a league or two from Lyons is so extensive, so picturesque, so enchantingly beautiful that, impatient as I was to enter the town, I could not refrain from stopping at a shabby little wine house and drinking coffee under the mulberry trees to enjoy the warm day, the cooling breeze, and the noble prospect which every way surrounded us.'

Lyons too was sheer delight. Here Thicknesse was particularly impressed by the little boats which taxied one across the Saône and Rhône. They were all rowed by female *patronnes*; 'yes, my dear sir, female!' wrote the Captain in one of his letters.

'Many of them are young, some very handsome, and all neatly dressed. I have more than once been disposed to blush when I saw a pretty woman sitting just opposite me labouring in an action which I thought would have been more becoming myself. I asked one of these female scullers how she got her bread in the winter.

' "Oh Sir," said she, giving me a very significant look – such a one as you can better conceive than I convey, "dans l'hiver j'ai un autre talent."

'And I can assure you I was glad she did not exercise both her talents at the same time of the year. Yet I could not refrain from giving her a double fee as I thought there was something due to her winter, as well as her summer abilities.'

In the same town a fine art dealer's, 'almost opposite the General Post Office where I went everyday for my letters', also claimed his attention. Thicknesse considered himself a fair judge of paintings and one of his most recent vendettas had been with Thomas Gainsborough. This well-publicised contretemps threatened to detract from the fact that he, Thicknesse, had been Gainsborough's discoverer. Twenty years previously he had stumbled upon the young artist in the provincial obscurity of Ipswich. He instantly recognised an exceptional talent, introduced his protégé to the best society of London and Bath, and so launched him on his dazzling career.

Hoping to uncover a French Gainsborough, the Captain browsed round the gallery in Lyons. The proprietor seemed disposed to help and asked his pretty assistant to show *monsieur* 'the little miniature'.

'She then opened a drawer and took out a book (I think it was her mass book), and brought me a picture so indecent that I defy the most debauched imagination to conceive anything more so; yet she gave it me with a seeming decent face and only observed that it was *bien fait*.'

There followed an invitation to visit another shop where, up several flights of stairs, the same fair assistant conducted him round a chintzy boudoir lined with pornographic canvasses. Thicknesse asked their prices, then felt duty bound to ask the young lady her own price. She was worth nothing, she told him, and without a flicker of embarrassment she continued to point out the merits of the pictures. 'I verily believe that the woman was so totally a stranger to sentiment or decency that she considered herself employed in the ordinary way of shopkeepers – that of shewing and selling her goods.'

With a fine eye for incident and detail, disarming candour, and much skill as a raconteur, the Captain was revealing himself as an exceptional travel writer. Reading his account of this journey even Dr Johnson would be impressed; it was both honest and entertaining, he told Boswell. The recognition and consequence which had so long eluded Thicknesse were within his grasp. But perhaps what emerges even more strongly is his sheer delight in each novelty. It is hard to believe that this is the same embittered man who had quarrelled away the last thirty-five years of his life. Under the stimulus of travel he was rediscovering his old, and infinitely more endearing self.

At Lyons the cabriolet was loaded onto the deck of a barge for the onward journey. Callee stayed in the shafts, the family kept their seats and Jocko his mount. Thus boldly silhouetted against the sunlit waters of the Rhône they whirled downstream towards Avignon. On their right lay Languedoc, 'a province', noted Thicknesse, 'in which £10,000 were lately distributed by the *sagacious* Chancellor of England among an hundred French peasants.' It was an unpleasant reminder. The £10,000 in question was the estate of his first wife's mother, a Huguenot. Thicknesse had claimed it as part of the daughter's dowry and had taken his case to the court of Chancery and then to the Lords. Their Lordships found against him, the money went to the deceased's Languedoc cousins, and Thicknesse stupidly wrote a string of libellous letters to the press criticising the judgement. It was this affair that had obliged him to seek refuge beyond the reach of British justice.

The proximity of these French beneficiaries would surely have prompted the Thicknesse of a few weeks before into a further display of pique. As it was, he was positively conciliatory. 'If the decision [of the Lords] had made one man wretched, it made the hearts of many glad; and I should be pleased to drink a bottle of wine with any of my fortunate cousins – and will, if I can find them out.' He did not find them out. Instead the Thicknesses joined a party of French officers for a gastronomic pilgrimage to the inn at Pont St Esprit. The *maître cuisinier* was unprepossessing but the meal turned out to be the best the Captain had ever tasted:

'The first appearance on the table was a fine large water melon, a salad, a basket of ripe figs, and some enormous bunches of black and white, or rather red and yellow grapes, between which were a boiled poularde and another fricasséed with six skewers of sweet bread most exquisitely dressed. Then followed a larded hare roasted, a roasted poularde, stewed pigeons, becca fica roasted [evidently warblers of some sort that had been fattened on figs], cream custard, roasted truffles and coffee.'

The next stop was Nîmes. Here the family whiled away a few happy days poking about among the Roman antiquities. Then on to Montpellier, famed for the culture of verdigris. This unusual industry the Captain investigated with great thoroughness. But he was disappointed by the town. A most unhealthy place, he thought; the 'musquitos' were worse even than in Jamaica. 'In spite of all the hostilities we committed upon them, they made our faces, hands and legs as bad in appearance as persons just recovering from the small-pox – and infinitely more miserable.' A liberal ministration of ointment of marshmallows brought a measure of relief.

The 'musquitos' continued troublesome until at last the Pyrenees – 'those adamantine hills' according to Thicknesse – hove into sight. Gushing waterfalls, craggy precipices, the humble homes of the goatherds – the Thicknesses were in raptures. But, as every traveller knows, the raptures do not last. The impertinence of the Spanish frontier guards knew no bounds. They presumed to enquire the nationality of the Thicknesses.

'Hottentot', declared the Captain, tendering his passport 'where I knew no information of that kind was given'. (It was evidently the height of vulgarity to have a passport that revealed anything as personal as the bearer's nationality.)

Instead the Captain treated his audience to a lecture on the Hottentot constitution; any residual doubts in the minds of the customs officers must have been dispelled by the obviously African origins of Jocko and the parakeet. 'But I soon found that these questions were leading to a more important one, and that was what *countryman* my horse was. For suspecting him to be an Englishman, they would, if I had owned it, have made me pay a considerable duty for his admission to Spain.'

Thicknesse preferred to offer a small douceur and the cabriolet was allowed to roll on down into Catalonia. The countryside continued beautiful, but quite different. 'The hogs, for instance, which are all white on the French side, are all black on this – as well as the men and the women.' The inns were more expensive, the fields less bountiful. But provisions were abundant and the midday picnic, or 'hedgedinner', remained a substantial affair. Eaten in some shady grove overlooking the Mediterranean it was the highlight of the travelling day. Callee would be watered and given a munch of hay, the girls would recline in the shade, Jocko could explore the olive trees and Mrs Thicknesse exercise on the viol. For the Captain it was a chance to meet the local peasantry. The Spanish were more reserved than the French, a fact which he ascribed to their scant acquaintance with Liberty. 'Oh Liberty, sweet Liberty,' he wrote, 'without thee life cannot be enjoyed, thou parent of comfort whose children bless thee though they dwell upon the barren rocks or the most surly region of the earth.' The unexpected implication of this outburst was that Liberty was to be found, par excellence, in England. Evidently the recollection of the last painful years had already dimmed. It was the first symptom of homesickness.

The Thicknesse narrative gives no dates but the family must now have been on the road for some four months and it was perhaps early October when they reached Barcelona. Here a most unfortunate episode occurred which nearly soured the whole Spanish experience. The Captain went to change some money with the British consul and was 'contunded' when this individual commenced a minute scrutiny of his bank notes. This was bad enough but when the consul's colleague presumed to question his very identity the Captain stormed out resolving to live on bread and water rather than submit to such impertinent scrutiny.

Unwittingly the consul and his friend had cut the Captain to the quick. Questioning his credit was like questioning the legitimacy of his birth. About nothing was he more sensitive than money. He had learnt his lesson in youth when unexpectedly posted to that captaincy in Jamaica. News of this appointment, of the higher salary it carried, and of the three months advance on it which he could draw before he left, had rendered him 'quite intoxicated'. He moved into smart lodgings, spent his evenings at 'a certain *female* coffee-house' and was excelling the rake's rate of progress. But late one night, tipping off his sedan chair carriers in a downpour, he inadvertently pressed on them twelve guineas instead of the fourpence intended. In the cold light of the following morning he grasped his breeches by the wrong end and, as the eight halfpennies rolled upon the floor, he realised he was broke at a stroke.

'This early disaster has put me upon my guard ever since about money matters, or I had probably continued to this day as indiscreet in that matter as I have in all other matters, for I know not any other folly I have guarded against.'

From Barcelona Thicknesse headed inland for the great monastic settlement of Montserrat where 'I am sure I will meet with more charity than I met with humanity or politeness in Barcelona'. He would not be disappointed. Montserrat was both the scenic and psychological climax of the whole journey.

Like the ostrich, Thicknesse had two methods of escape. One was to run – to travel or emigrate. The other was to bury himself in rural seclusion. This showed itself in a passion for hermitages, derelict barns and ruined cottages. Once he had made one habitable he would commence the construction of grottoes, bowers and summer-houses in the neighbouring woods. Perhaps it was just further evidence of that 'romantic turn' which had led him to build his shack on an island in the Savannah river. Or perhaps it was some form of agoraphobia. At all events it predisposed him towards the mountain of Montserrat, honeycombed with hermits' cells. At an inn at the bottom of the mountain the cabriolet was unloaded, Callee was put out to grass, and the family took to their legs. For what may have been several weeks they trailed up and down the rock-cut staircases. They collected wild-flowers, stalked the ever more sensational panoramas, and flushed out the hermits. The Captain was in his element. Not only was it the most charming spot he had ever seen but the monks were the saintliest community on earth. He tried to buy his own plot of land, he was half persuaded to adopt Catholicism, and he certainly compiled the most exhaustive and detailed guide to the place. Montserrat was by no means his personal discovery, but to his contemporaries it was probably as remote and exotic as today are the monasteries of Lhasa.

With the onset of winter the tourists reluctantly withdrew and, giving Barcelona a wide berth, returned to France. Christmas was spent at Perpignan and the new year at Montpellier where they arrived after dark and in the midst of a cloudburst. The Captain had to lead Callee while feeling for the edge of the road with his stick. It was the most fraught occasion he could recall. 'No, not even at the bar of the House of Lords did I dread the danger so much as the idea of tumbling my family over a precipice without the power to assist them, or if they were *gone*, resolution enough to *follow them.*'

The rest of the winter was spent in further archaeological rambles in Provence; the Captain was particularly keen on collecting inscriptions – a good excuse to air his Latin. In Marseilles the delicate business of changing money went off as smoothly as he could have wished, but at Nîmes, betraying an old weakness, he challenged his host to a duel. At stake was not the man's mistress, an eighteen-year-old of exceptional beauty who dressed as a *garçon* and was surely worth a fight, but rather the right to use the kitchen of the house. It was an absurd quarrel and the Captain was flabbergasted when the Frenchman actually accepted his challenge. With considerable loss of face he beat a hasty retreat. Spring was on hand, the roads were drying out, and it was safe to head north again.

Near Avignon they passed a dancing bear who, like Callee, was being ridden by a larger version of Jocko. The Captain reined in and went to inspect.

'As it was upon the high road I desired leave to present Jocko to his grandfather (for so he appeared both in age and size). The interview, though they were both males, was very affecting. Never did a father receive a long lost child with more seeming affection than did the old gentleman my Jocko; he embraced him with every degree of tenderness imaginable, while the young gentleman (like other gentlemen of the present age) betrayed a perfect indifference. In my conscience, I believe there was some consanguinity between them, or the reception would have proved more mutual.'

The reference here was to the Captain's own less than affectionate sons. George and Philip Touchet – significantly they had taken their mother's surname – clearly found their eccentric father an embarrassment. George had inherited a baronetcy, also through his mother, and this, from the Captain's point of view, exacerbated matters. But the root cause of their quarrel had as so often to do with money. A certain sum had changed hands. The boys thought it was part of their patrimony, the father claimed it was a loan. When he asked for it back his letters went unanswered. Eventually he had recourse to the only weapon he knew and published a pamphlet on the affair. Further evidence of his displeasure may be found in a clause in his will whereby he asked that his right hand should be cut off and presented to George 'to remind him of his duty to God, after so long having abandoned the duty he owed to his father'.

By about June the family were back at Lyons whence they continued to retrace their steps northward. The Captain could be infuriatingly vague about dates but when occasion demanded he could be explicit enough about places:

'Post House, St George, Six leagues from Lyons.

'I am particular in dating this letter in the hopes that every English traveller may avoid the place I write from by either stopping short or going beyond it, as it is . . . the worst I have met with in my whole journey. We came in early in the afternoon and while I was in the courtyard I saw a flat basket stand upon the ground the bottom of which was covered with boiled spinage [*sic*]. As my dog and several others in the yard had often put their noses into it I concluded it was put down for *their* food, not mine, till I saw a dirty girl patting it into round balls and two children playing with it, one of whom, *to lose no time*, was performing *an office* that none could *do for her.*

'I asked the maid what she was about and what it was she was so preparing. She told me it was spinage. "Not for me I hope," said I. "Oui, pour vous et le monde." I then forbad her bringing any to table and put the little girl *off her centre* by an angry push. . . . Nevertheless, with my entrée, came up a dish of this *delicate spinage*, with which I made the girl a very pretty *Chapeau Anglais*, for I turned it, dish and all upon her head.'

It was a good story and Thicknesse was quite sure that, though the French nation might blush to hear of such an insanitary *auberge*, 'the truth justifies it and I hope the publication may amend it.' This was invariably his attitude. The good news must always be balanced by the bad. If there were places that merited commendation there must be others which it was the traveller's duty to condemn. Auxerre for instance, where the two Thicknesse girls were deposited in a convent, was delightful; Paris, though, was not. 'To a person of fortune in the heyday of life Paris may be preferable to London. But to one of my age and walk of life it is the least agreeable place I have seen in France.' The streets were dangerous, the shops expensive, and it was impossible 'to get amongst the first people so as to be admitted to their suppers'.

The Captain had made a brief visit to Paris in 1766 but the only change in ten years was that the cobbled *pavé* of the streets seemed to have worn smoother. This was some consolation to old bones; but he did not regard it as an improvement. The combination of springless cabriolet and the roughest road surface was, he maintained, a guarantee of good health. It was a form of exercise, it assisted the digestion, and above all, it was a sure remedy for gallstones.

Gallstones were a subject about which the Captain spoke with feeling – so much so, and so often, that he had once been nick-named Governor Gallstone. Since his twenties he had been plagued by this most painful affliction and on one agonising occasion in the 1740s had passed a grand total of twenty-seven, 'the smallest of which was the size of a large coffee berry and some double that size'. The gallstone in its natural state he believed to be a knobbly accretion like a mulberry. To render it smooth and easily passable it needed a good jolting either in a carriage or, better still, on horseback. A sustained and excruciating trot was the ideal. When Lord Thurlow, Chancellor in Lord North's ministry, betrayed symptoms similar to his own he strongly recommended this drastic treatment and was pleased to report its complete success. 'His Lordship . . . trotted himself from that day on and, in a few weeks, had so well recovered as to desire all my family to eat a parting dinner with him before he left Bath.'

Rubbed and jolted to the smoothness of peas the stones were best passed while under a sedative of opium. From his days as an apothecary's apprentice Thicknesse knew that most patent medicines were useless. The agony of gallstones merited something stronger and only opium, taken in alarming quantities, fitted the bill. The fact that it was addictive need not cause alarm. 'By having been compelled to make use of opium in my youth, I now find it necessary in age and seldom miss it a single day. . . . It gives me spirits by day and by night a kind of quiet repose rather than sleep.'

The 'first cordial in nature', together with the heavy doses of purgatives which he considered equally essential, must also have had some effect on his unpredictable temperament. A year of travel, the happiest in his life, had revealed the Captain in a sympathetic light and had supposedly given him 'that peace of mind which no earthly power can despoil me of'. But it had not changed him. He would soon be cutting as cantankerous a figure as ever in English society. From Paris the Thicknesses headed back to Calais and, after receiving assurances that no action was pending against him, the Captain returned to England in late 1776.

A plan to visit Italy in the following year was abandoned and for the next six years he lived at 'St Catherine's Hermitage' in the hills above Bath. The Hermitage, his pride and joy, was little more than a ramshackle hut; it had a gigantic oak tree growing through the kitchen, and his cabriolet, 'fast fixt and never more to move', supported one of the walls. But it was within easy reach of the coffee-houses of Bath, it had a 'noble prospect' to remind him of Montserrat, and if Mrs Thicknesse preferred to live more comfortably in town, no doubt Callee and Jocko appreciated it. (The parakeet, incidentally, had come to an unfortunate end in Calais. It was shut in a cupboard at the Hôtel d'Angleterre and – quite by accident according to the Captain – a lively terrier was shut in the same cupboard; the terrier was found but only a few feathers of the parakeet remained.)

At St Catherine's Hermitage he wrote the narrative of his journey; it was published in 1777 and became an instant success. A second and third edition quickly followed and by the time the Thicknesses again ventured abroad it had been translated into French and German. This second tour was in 1782–3 and took them across the Pays Bas (Belgium) to Aix-la-Chapelle and back. It was an altogether more modest affair; the route was well known and without Jocko or Callee the Thicknesse party cut a less dashing figure. It did, however, make another highly successful book and again it convinced the Captain that travel was the answer to all his problems.

In 1791 he paid another visit to Paris. He was now a remarkable seventy-two and Paris had at last changed. But ever sympathetic to the down-trodden, and especially the French peasants, he welcomed the Revolution and resolved to return again in 1792 en route, at last, to Italy.

'If God delights so much in variety, as all things animate and inanimate sufficiently prove, no wonder that man should do so too: and I have now been so accustomed to move, though slowly, that I intend to creep on to *my journey's end*, by which means I may live to have been an inhabitant of every town almost in Europe, and die as I have lately (and wish I had always) lived, a free citizen of the whole world, slave to no sect nor subject to any king.'

In November 1792 he died, appropriately enough, on the Paris stage-coach a little south of Boulogne with Mrs Thicknesse sitting beside him.

It would be kind to end the story there; but, as the Captain himself always protested when about to deliver some particularly damning accusation, truth demands that the full story be told. The decade and a half between his journey to Spain and his death had seen him involved in more quarrels than ever. The reputation that came with his travelogues did not assuage his prickly nature but merely lent weight to his polemics. Nor were the travelogues his only publications. There was a spate of scurrilous pamphlets and, most important of all, there was his three-volume *Memoirs and Anecdotes*.

This extraordinary work, published when the author was in his seventies, was supposedly designed to rebut some libellous accusations made by two of his deadliest enemies; one, a doctor, claimed that the Captain had been guilty of cowardice whilst in Jamaica some fifty years before, and the other, a naval captain and accomplice of the doctor's, presumed to challenge Thicknesse to a duel although himself eighty-one, deaf and lame. Thicknesse preferred to deal with them in print and in page upon page of invective and heavily italicised innuendo spared neither their years nor their morals. Perceiving, in the process, that slander and scurrility sold books, he widened the scope of the work to include all his enemies, past and present. Although structured like an autobiography it reads more like a *Private Eye* omnibus. The Captain could be perceptive as well as trivial and funny as well as cruel.

Happily too, he does betray a hint of remorse. At the very end of volume three, with less than a year to live, he looks back on 'a long and chequered career' and 'can only wonder at my own folly in thinking it worthwhile to have contested with knaves and fools'. For more than half a century he had been wondering at the childishness of other men's pursuits. Now suddenly he wondered at his own and, remembering his old friends the American Indians, ended his literary career with a unique but not untypical confession:

'Had that incomprehensible *Being* who ordained animation to me, condescended to have consulted my spirit about which race of mortal men I would have chosen to have been clothed with flesh among, I would have preferred the Indian cast of existence to any I have hitherto met with among civilised society.'

2
'I Anxious'
Thomas Manning

In late March 1808 the *Discovery*, a survey ship of the Honourable
East India Company, approached the unexplored Paracel Islands
in the middle of the South China Sea. On board, Lieutenant Ross
and his men must have scanned the coastline with relish; where
better to spend a few weeks with gun and compass than this island
paradise? Not so, though, their solitary passenger. Thomas Manning, scholar, wit, and now reluctant traveller, paced the decks in
his long Chinese robes and stroked his mighty beard. He was
wasting precious time. The islands, indeed exploring trips in
general, were a grievous bore. The coral reefs, the sand bars, the
rolling breakers – all was 'hideous deformity'. Turtles wallowed in
the shallows, and the sea-birds were so disgustingly tame they
would not get off their nests.

To make matters worse, the islands proved far from uninhabited. On the first islet they found a wrecked junk with its crew of
no less than 561 persons encamped in great misery on the shore.
'We saved them all,' noted Manning laconically. 'Their gratitude
was unspeakable.' So was the subsequent overcrowding on the
Discovery. Lieutenant Ross must discharge his unexpected cargo
as rapidly as possible; he could then return to the islands. Accordingly, he sailed for the nearest mainland port, Tourane (Da Nang)
on the coast of Cochin-China (Vietnam). Manning perked up. He
could not have planned things better. His Vietnamese costume
was ready, his trunks packed, and with luck he would soon be
making his way north into China proper.

'I shall soon see the Emperor and shall perhaps feel his pulse!
What stories I shall have to tell! And who knows but – aye, aye, – in
short – however. If you see any of my friends tell them I'm off and
in good spirits.'

He was writing to his dearest friend, the essayist Charles Lamb.
The two men had first met ten years earlier at Cambridge when
they were both in their mid-twenties. Lamb, who already

belonged to that literary circle which included Wordsworth, Coleridge and Southey, was immediately impressed. A brilliant academic, the tall, sombre-looking Manning refused to take any-thing, least of all his genius, seriously. Like a Shakespearean fool his conversation was a staunchless flow of pun and parody, of Latin quips, outlandish howls and endearing soliloquies. 'He is a man in a thousand,' declared Lamb, 'an enchanter almost, far beyond Coleridge in power of impressing.' But he was also chronically lazy and seldom exerted this power of imagination. 'If he did, I know of no man of genius at all comparable to him.' Very definitely, Lamb was the disciple, Manning the master.

At the time Manning was teaching mathematics. His standard introduction to algebra had just been published and was soon to be followed by the revelation of a new way of computing logar-ithms. Originally he had been a classical scholar but having exhausted Greek and Latin, and now algebra and arithmetic, his formidable intelligence sought a new and still more challenging discipline. Chinese – not just the language but the whole literature and civilisation of China – provided the answer.

There was, of course, a problem here. In 1800 oriental studies were in their infancy. Eight years earlier the first British mission to Peking had been unable to find a single European who could act as interpreter; eventually they had had to send to Rome where a Chinese Christian, who was studying for the priesthood and could therefore translate from Chinese into Latin, was recruited. It was probably this mission, and the mass of miscellaneous information it brought back, which first roused Manning's interest. But in 1800 there was still no one at Cambridge who could read Chinese. Paris was the centre for oriental studies and Manning duly entrusted himself to Napoleon's France. Three years later England and France went to war. All English residents and travellers were promptly interned – all, that is, except Manning. So high stood his reputation amongst French orientalists and mathematicians that a special petition was sent to Napoleon. The emperor personally signed his passport – the only instance of such a favour to an enemy national – and Manning was free to leave.

The passport was to enable him to proceed direct to China. He had now outgrown the sinological nursery of Paris and was determined to pursue his studies at their source. Lamb was horrified; he desperately tried to dissuade him. The 'enchanter' was succumbing to his own fertile imagination. 'Pray try and cure yourself. Take hellebore. Pray to avoid the fiend. Read no more books of voyages; they are nothing but lies.' To the extent that

Manning abandoned his idea of proceeding direct to China over-land through Russia, this appeal may have succeeded. But he was not in the habit of listening to advice. His heart was set on China, and for the next twelve years no one, be he emperor or mandarin, governor-general or bosom friend, was going to sidetrack him. 'My ideas refuse any other channel . . . the moment I set myself down to anything quietly, in comes Independent Tartary [China].'

He returned to London. The East India Company maintained a much harassed trading establishment at Canton on which he had now set his sights. He studied medicine at the Westminster Hospital, won the support of that arch entrepreneur of explo-ration, Sir Joseph Banks, and was duly appointed physician to the Canton merchants. He sailed from Portsmouth in May 1806.

'For God's sake, don't think any more of Independent Tartary,' Lamb had pleaded. Now he was reduced to tears. It was like parting with someone on the scaffold. Would they ever meet again: 'O Manning, I am serious to sinking almost . . .' Manning, though, was far from serious:

'I am not dead or dying – some people go into Yorkshire for four years and never come to London all the while! I go to China. What's the difference to our London friends?

'I am persuaded I shall come back and see more of you than I have ever been able. Who knows but I may make a fortune and take you and Mary [Lamb's sister] a-riding in my coach . . . Of course you know you must leave room for my little Chinese wife, because poor pipsey's feet are so small she can't walk, you know.

'Does a man at my age forget and neglect his dearest friends? No. Well then you and Mary are safe – so God bless you both.

'Writing does me hurt at present. My throat now begins to be sore, and I have no currant jelly aboard.'

In 1806 the Chinese empire was as firmly closed to foreigners as Communist China in the 1960s. Manning's first hope of gaining admittance was as a man of medicine and science (the Chinese were thought to have a passion for scientific gimmickry). As soon as he arrived, therefore, he drafted a petition to the emperor volunteering his services as astronomer and physician. The petition probably never left Canton. Servants of the East India Company were not only forbidden to travel inland but were not even allowed into the city. Their only dealings with the Chinese were with the local mandarins who, jealous of their lucrative offices, frustrated all contacts with Peking.

It was even illegal for a subject of the Celestial Empire to divulge to the barbarian outsiders the secrets of his mother tongue. Manning got round this by enlisting a Chinese from Macao as his tutor. But progress was slow. If it was the structure of the language which had at first fascinated him, now it was the learning which he glimpsed behind it. In recommending 'this very amiable young man' to the East India Company, Sir Joseph Banks had contrasted his energetic mind with the mildness of his character. Mild, aloof, or simply lazy, Manning sensed in Chinese culture a refined civility and an urbane wisdom which matched his own inclinations. To the dismay of his worthy compatriots he adopted Chinese dress and grew a long, and then most unfashionable, beard. It was not a question of compromising. He wanted not so much to study the Chinese way of life as to experience and absorb it.

After a year of unsuccessfully trying to sway the Cantonese mandarins, Manning saw in Lieutenant Ross's expedition to the Paracels a totally new line of attack. Even without evacuating wrecked junks, the expedition was going to have to touch on the coast of Cochin-China to reprovision. Manning would simply disembark there and make his way north into the Chinese province of Yunnan. Everything would, of course, depend on his being able to pass himself off – beard and all – as a Chinese, or at least a Cochin-Chinese. Fine featured and full lipped he might have passed as a Spanish grandee but, according to a contemporary, looked 'as little like a Tartar as any son of Adam one might meet in London'.

In the event the disguise was not to be tested. Within hours of reaching Tourane, the *Discovery* was heading back for the Paracels with an irate Manning still on board. Sadly, the letter which relates what went wrong is lost. 'We went too late,' he writes elsewhere. 'Dringle-dringle. No time to manage matters on shore and other unlucky circumstances . . . I saw a little of the villages on the coast of Cochin-China, but that was not my object. I lost my time – I can hardly bear even now to think of it with patience.'

He was back in Canton, grappling again with 'the veil'd mysteries of the Chinese language' and reading Lamb's just published *Tales from Shakespeare.* He was also intrigued by a more ponderous work entitled *An Account of an Embassy to the Court of the Teshoo Lama.* The 'Teshoo Lama' was the Panchen Lama of Tashilunpo in Southern Tibet and the mission, led by Samuel Turner, a nephew of Warren Hastings, the first Governor-General of India, had travelled from Calcutta to Tibet by way of Bhutan in the Himalayas. It was all of twenty-five years ago and since then subsequent missions to Tibet had invariably failed to reach their destination. But Manning, with the boundless optimism of a man astride his pet obsession, was not going to be put off easily.

He arrived in Calcutta, still dressed as a Chinese but with a year's more beard, in 1810. A letter from the Select Committee in Canton recommended him as eminently qualified for exploring China and solicited the Governor-General's assistance. Unfortunately the Governor-General was not especially interested in China. Nor was he any too sure about Manning. The outlandish appearance, the affectation of superiority, and the spate of banter went down well enough in the racier fringes of Calcutta society. But there must be something fundamentally unsound about a man who insisted on worshipping in Hindu temples. For the upright *sahibs*, who pushed pens and pursued promotion, the impertinent traveller seemed to harbour a withering contempt; he kept lecturing them on the unsuitability of their dress. It was none of his business and no way to set about getting a diplomatic commission.

Empty-handed, therefore, short of funds, alone but for his Chinese servant, unarmed, and blissfully ignorant of what lay in store, Thomas Manning rode out of Calcutta and headed for the Himalayas. As the crow flies the distance to Peking must be about three thousand miles. Turner, and his predecessor George Bogle, were the only Europeans to have crossed the Himalayas and entered Tibet. But this represented only the first five hundred miles; and though both men had tried, neither had got as far as the Tibetan capital. Manning proposed to follow their route through Bhutan and then strike out across the mountains to Lhasa. There he hoped to join one of the periodical caravans which tackled the frigid wastes of central Tibet. And so to China. It was surely one of the most fantastic and impractical schemes in the history of exploration. To make matters worse, Manning had got his timing all wrong; he would enter the eastern Himalayas while they were still being deluged by the monsoon, and reach Lhasa in time to sample the rigours of a Tibetan winter. Then there was the political situation in Tibet, which could hardly have been less favourable; Chinese influence was stronger, more pervasive and more exclusive than in Turner's day.

And, finally, there was Manning himself, desperately impractical, far from robust and hating every minute of it. A more reluctant and incompetent traveller never ventured abroad. His journal, such as it is, may be regarded as an example of the anti-travelogue.

No stirring evocations of landscape here, no detailed observations of society. Dates occur, spasmodically, bearings and distances never. Of variety and challenge – the very spice of travel – there is little. Instead he dwells on the monotony and discomforts; his narrative becomes a whimsical catalogue of petty frustrations.

And yet the man is hard to resist. The journal was never meant for publication and it retains an intimacy, which does him no discredit, and an immediacy which is rare indeed in nineteenth-century travelogues. Invariably he writes at his own expense, but without the contrived levity of his letters to Lamb. The result may have been useless as a contribution to exploration, but it speaks volumes for the extraordinary character of its author.

'Just going to leave Calcutta for God knows where,' he wrote to Lamb. 'Very strange in mind – cannot write.' Nor did he. Neither Lamb nor anyone else heard tell of Manning for the next year. He left Calcutta in the summer of 1811, entered Bhutan in early September, and was soon climbing through the rank vegetation of the eastern Himalayas. After three days the path plunged into a torrent and – 'an unexpected trouble' – the guides advised him that horses could go no further. There followed a mile's trudge up the bed of the torrent and then the first serious climb. Footsore and far from fit, Manning 'toiled up slowly and with considerable difficulty'. His Chinese companion fared worse and reached the top suffering from 'palpitations and eruptions'. 'I told him it would do him good and prevent fever. Next day I bargained for people to carry us in chairs.'

Whether the Bhutanese would stand for this is not clear, but certainly within a week the travellers were back on their own feet. It was now Manning's turn to collapse with palpitations; he cured himself with stewed turnips, a humble dish but one which he held in high esteem. To reach Paro-dzong, the most important Bhutanese fort on their route, they climbed again. 'I find going uphill does not agree with me, perhaps because naturally I am going downhill.' By way of compensation, vistas of grandeur should now have been opening on all sides. Manning's failure to mention them is not significant. Typically he was far more concerned about the dismal weather. 'Wet, wet, always rain', and next day 'wet above, wet below, hard stones all the way'. Dripping and sodden he squelched into Paro-dzong and was lodged in a windowless and smoke-filled guardhouse.

Here, if his dates are anything to go by, he was detained for nearly a month. Lengthy negotiations with the Bhutanese were to be expected. Their chronic feuding, combined with awe of the

Chinese in Tibet and distrust of the British in India, had aborted most of the previous attempts to cross the mountains. Manning's disguise clearly did not fool them and, from later references in his story, we know that he too experienced his share of harassment and extortion. But he was allowed to proceed. Perhaps his smattering of Cantonese, and the undeniably Chinese character of his companion, convinced their captors that this unlikely duo belonged north of the mountains rather than south.

Manning quickly forgot both trials and triumphs in what appeared to him a far more testing affair. This was the famous case of the silver spoons, an incident magnified into an epic, which so rankled in Manning's mind that it overshadowed the crossing of the Himalayas. At the first camp out of Paro-dzong he discovered that, in place of his two silver spoons, he now had two pewter ones. Immediately he pointed the finger at his Chinese tutor, who had charge of such things, and at their Bhutanese guide. 'I told them I would not go on till I got my spoons.' The suspects prevaricated. It was four miles back to Paro; they would prefer to send someone to make the necessary enquiries and he would no doubt catch them up later. This, Manning insisted, would not do; 'I was obstinate.' The morning slipped by and at last the Bhutanese trudged back to the fort. He returned triumphantly bearing two spoons. But on inspection only one proved to be silver. Manning exploded. He would have the other or go back himself and lodge an official complaint. The Chinese, visibly shaken by this most uncharacteristic outburst, persuaded his accomplice to set off again, and by nightfall Manning had his precious spoons. 'It was not the value', he explained, 'but the principle. I am in bad, bad hands.'

Relations between Manning and his employees would continue to rank as a major preoccupation. Leadership was yet another of those traveller's qualities which he conspicuously lacked. His Chinese companion, seeing him being unmercifully fleeced in Paro, no doubt thought that a little subterfuge over a couple of spoons would go unnoticed. He mistook his man; this was precisely the sort of minor irritation which Manning could not stomach. In matters of consequence he could be docile to the point of servility; but, take this docility for granted, and suddenly he would pounce on a trifle and insist, against all reason, on having his way.

Unfortunately this petulance was more than matched by a moody streak in his companion. The day after the affair of the spoons, 'the Chinaman' was 'as cross as the devil' and refused to speak. Manning tried to ignore him and concentrate on his own predicament:

'Snow-fall in sight. Charming weather. Strange sensation coming along; warm and comfortable. Horse walking in a lane between two stone walls. The snow! Where am I? How can I be come here? Not a soul to speak to. I wept almost through excess of sensation, not grief.'

But the Chinaman's sullen gloom was getting him down. 'A spaniel would be better company.' That night he made careful enquiries. It appeared that the man had fallen off his horse and, though unhurt, was mortally offended that Manning had not attempted to console him. 'I did not see it.'

Two days later they reached the gaunt fortress of Phari-dzong. Manning fails to mention that they were now on Tibetan soil; he was far too preoccupied with his still sulking companion. After a visit to the local magistrate he sought to humour him. 'Was that a bird at the magistrate's which flapped so loud?' 'What signifies it whether it was a bird or not?' snapped the Chinese.

'Where he sat I thought he might see it; and I was curious to know if such large birds frequented the building. These are the answers I get. He is always discontented and grumbling, and takes no trouble off my hands. Being younger and, like all Asiatics, able to stoop and crouch without pain or difficulty, he might assist me in many things without trouble to himself. A younger brother, or any English young gentleman, would in his place of course lay the cloth, and do other little services when I am tired; but he does not seem to have much of the generous about him, nor does he in any way serve me, or behave to me with any show of affection or goodwill; consequently I grow no more attached to him than the first day I saw him. I could not have thought it possible to live so long with anyone without either disliking him or caring sixpence for him. He has good qualities too. The strangeness of his situation may partly excuse him.'

The strangeness of the man's situation was evident from the difficulty Manning had in defining it. Sometimes he refers to him as a servant or slave, at others as *munshi* (teacher or interpreter). It appears that this was the same Chinese whom he had originally employed as tutor in Canton. No wonder the poor man baulked at having to double as valet. Nor was this all. Manning's mastery of Chinese etiquette and idiom was still inadequate. In Phari-dzong he shunned two 'idle fellows' who turned out to be the fort's highest dignitaries and mistook their manservant for a girl. The job of smoothing over such *faux pas* fell to the Chinaman and the more they encountered Chinese influence, the more responsible and dangerous this liaison role became.

On October 27th news arrived that a Chinese border patrol was about to descend on Phari-dzong. Manning was hustled from his guest room and dumped in an altogether less satisfactory apartment. 'The new room had dirty floors and was rather cold.' It also had to double as their kitchen. 'Dirt, dirt, grease, smoke. Misery, but good mutton.' Four days later the patrol duly arrived. It was accompanied by a mandarin to whom Manning immediately sent his Chinaman. Next day he himself, clutching two bottles of cherry brandy and a wineglass, went to pay his respects. Much would depend on this meeting with such a high dignitary; but he was determined not to demean himself. 'Some of his [the mandarin's] people said I could not sit down before him. In that case I should not have gone.'

Fortunately the cherry brandy proved so acceptable that any lack of polish in the guest was overlooked. The mandarin, or 'general' as he was now called, turned out to be a most genial companion exuding that urbanity which Manning so admired. What a contrast to the dirty and ruffianly Tibetans. 'Things are much pleasanter now the Chinese are here.' The soldiers kept him well supplied with vegetables, the mandarin raised no objection to his opening an out-patients clinic, and there was even talk of how trade across the Himalayas might be improved. It was the East India Company's enthusiasm for such trade which had inspired the previous attempts to enter Tibet. In this respect they had all failed dismally; but here at last was an Englishman ideally situated to do something about it. Except that he was totally unprepared.

'I cannot help exclaiming in my mind (as I often do) what fools the Company are to give me no commission, no authority, no instructions. What use are their embassies when their ambassador cannot speak to a soul . . . No finesse, no tournure, no compliments. Fools, fools, fools, to neglect an opportunity they may never have again.'

His medicines were doing 'wonderfully well'. His patients – mostly Chinese soldiers – petitioned that he be allowed to accompany the patrol to Gyantse, and the general agreed. 'This is very pleasant.' Gyantse was on the road to Lhasa and, as part of the general's entourage, Manning would travel in safety and even with a degree of comfort. Things were going every bit as smoothly as his ill-founded optimism had anticipated. He could afford to cock a snook at the stuffy *sahibs* of the Calcutta bureaucracy.

Accordingly, on November 5th, he prepared to leave Phari-dzong with the Chinese patrol. New snow lay all around and a sharp frost had frozen the general's wine in its bottles. Manning bethought himself of his ice-skates. Skating was one of his few recorded pastimes and, by his own account, he was remarkably good at it. He had actually had the forethought to bring his skates and now happily anticipated a chance to exhibit his skill.

At dawn they all scampered off across the plain. After a good mutton lunch with the general they slowed to a trot; and by the end of the day were trudging along in the teeth of an icy gale. Manning had foolishly packed his sheepskin, and tottered into camp with a high fever. Next day the wind had dropped but he found himself allotted a particularly ferocious horse. It bit, kicked and finally bolted. Beard flying and long legs dangling in the useless stirrups, Manning sawed at the bridle; he was only saved by a herd of yaks obligingly blocking the path. Much shaken, he abandoned the idea of skating for that day and turned in early.

This billet was a single large room, 'low, long, dark, narrow, black, windowless and full of smoke'.

'There seemed to be several families belonging to it and at night several women and girls came in, who undressed themselves in the sides, and spread their beds long after I was laid down and quiet. I now and then took an impertinent peek, but the smoke was so thick and the light so bad that I could discern nothing.'

He slept in his clothes as usual; 'it was a great trouble to me', he explained, 'to undo my bedding.' But he was already in two minds about this slovenliness. Little insects, whom he would not name and to whose society he was not accustomed, were taking unfair advantage of it. Next day he could stand it no longer. Throwing caution to the icy wind he stripped off and systematically 'dismissed as many of my retinue as I could get sight of'. 'I shall say no more of them than that I did not get thoroughly rid of them until some time after my arrival at Lhasa.'

He still desperately needed a valet. By chance, it happened that the general had just such a man. At least he had in tow one Sid, a Chinese with a surely unusual Chinese name, to whom he owed a favour. Initially Sid was recommended as a cook. Manning, who reckoned that he had a most discriminating palate – as well as a liking for Chinese cuisine – agreed to pay his rather exorbitant salary. Come breakfast next morning 'Sid . . . brought me a cup of stewed lights'. He wanted to ingratiate himself, explained Manning who, however discriminating his palate, must have had an exceptionally obliging digestion. Later he conceded that Sid's activities in the kitchen were not so commendable; 'he does not understand even the elements of his profession.' He was also 'a notorious scamp' with a full share of impudence. But he had one redeeming feature. Like all Chinese he was expert at little domestic offices – laundry work, stitching, hammering nails and wrapping up parcels. They must learn these things in infancy, thought Manning.

'For my part I never could to this day fold up a shirt or other vestment. A handkerchief or sheet I can manage, but nothing further; everything else I roll up, so that if I had to put together my Chinese dresses after I had dried them, I should have made a very clumsy parcel.'

Sometime in mid-November (dates disappear completely at this stage of the journal) the general and his entourage reached Gyantse. Like most Tibetan towns it was impressive enough from a distance but did not bear close inspection. The streets were deep in mud and the tall white houses dirtier and draughtier than stables. Manning, the *munshi* and Sid were lodged at the local mandarin's house which proved to be an oasis of Chinese civilisation and comfort. The windows were papered, the folding doors adorned with paintings, and the Chinese soldiery kept them well supplied with delicacies from the mandarin's kitchen.

Manning immediately wrote to Lhasa for permission to proceed there. While he awaited a reply, he set up a surgery and cultivated his Chinese hosts. A case of 'intermittent fever' was cured with a dose of 'opium, Fowler's arsenic powder and a few papers of [quinine] bark'. Another patient was so grateful for a course of antimony that he went down on his knees and bowed to the ground before the foreigner. Business was such that again there was no time to exhibit his expertise on the ice.

No less satisfactory were his essays into Chinese society. The sub-mandarin declared Manning's beard the finest he had ever seen, and the general invited him to a musical evening during which both host and guest performed on the flute. 'I tried a few country dances but perceived that that quick kind of music was not very gratifying to their ears.' Only on the domestic front were stresses still evident. The arrival of Sid had done nothing to mollify the *munshi*; he was as moody and unpredictable as ever. When a patient described his symptoms more than once – and according to Manning, patients always described their symptoms more than once – the *munshi*, acting as interpreter, flew off the handle. It transpired that his sensitive nature simply could not abide any form of repetition. Looking back over past quarrels, Manning thought this explained a lot and resolved to be particularly circumspect in future.

But the *munshi* went on sulking; and next day, over some trifle, he again exploded 'with such bitterness and fury as was scarcely endurable'. Manning plucked up all his courage and determined to speak out.

'I begged of him not to eat me up . . . and lamented my ill luck in having with me a person to whom I was so afraid of putting a question that I was perpetually deterred; it being necessary for me first to go round about, and with civil speech and preface, bring him into the humour to listen to it and answer.'

The *munshi* met this attack 'without much asperity', indeed with a rather pathetic enquiry as to why, in that case, Manning had brought him along. He might also have mentioned – although Manning must have known this – that the risk he was taking was considerably greater than his master's. And so it would prove. For one thing, any subject of the Celestial Empire who went abroad without permission could expect to be penalised on his return. But this was as nothing compared to the unspecified punishments that might be meted out if the man he was bringing back with him should prove to be an undesirable or a spy. The prospect of being held responsible for the erratic Manning must have loomed all too large on his horizon. And when eventually there arrived permission – or was it a command? – to proceed to Lhasa, the *munshi*'s irritable and gloomy forebodings were understandable.

Parting from the general with genuine regret, Manning, the *munshi* and Sid embarked on the last and most challenging leg of the journey to Lhasa. They were now alone but for the Tibetan guides, it was at least late November, and ahead lay some of the highest passes on their whole route. Moreover Gyantse was as far into Tibet as any of the previous missions from India had got. Manning was out on his own, not just a traveller but a pioneer. Perhaps in recognition on this, his journal actually includes a few topographical details. For two days they followed the Gyantse river upstream stopping by night at the Chinese post houses. The luggage was carried on yaks and, as they climbed ever higher, Manning congratulated himself on his new winter wardrobe. This had been made by the military tailor in Gyantse and consisted of sheepskin stockings and boots, a long, incredibly heavy sheepskin lined robe, a fur tippet and a quilted cap with ear flaps. The Chinese might laugh, but at least he was spared from frostbite.

On the third day the cold became excessive. A night in the open would now have meant certain death. The wind howled across the wintry wastes and Manning's beard tinkled with icicles. They passed a glacier 'which descended down to the level of the road' and they wound through some lofty snow-covered mountains. This must have been the Karo La (Pass), some 17,000 feet above sea level. Manning, of course, never bothered with altitudes, although one might have expected some mention of respiratory problems. Elsewhere he had complained of breathlessness but ascribed it to the smoke-filled interiors of the Tibetan houses.

The next day brought them down to the shores of an extensive lake, presumably the Yamdrok Tso. This they skirted for three days. No provisions were available but they still had 'a piece of excellent pickled pork that the general had given us for prog on the road'. Manning had a passion for pig meat. It prompted him to write one of the best celebrations of pig killing in the English language and it inspired Lamb's famous *Dissertation upon Roast Pig*. As the two Chinese wandered off in search of some cheerless, doorless shed for the night's rest, and the sun set across the lake in a blaze of icy glory, Manning chewed a delicious knob of ham.

'Turning my head back towards the west, I had a noble view of a set of snowy mountains collected into focus, as it were; their summits empurpled with the evening sun and their majestic, graceful forms ever varying as I advanced into new positions. Though I kept a long, lingering eye upon them, yet I heartily wished that I might never see them again. My lips almost spontaneously pronounced this wish repeatedly, as I apostrophised them in my mind. Fruitless wish!'

Somewhere, behind the captious aesthete and the bantering scholar, lurked a genuine romantic. Charles Lamb would have found it hard to credit, but Charles Lamb was a long way away. The cruel, empty landscapes of Tibet and the strange unreality of his own situation were working a subtle change in Manning. When the luckless Sid carelessly smashed his china cups, he scarcely reacted; two months earlier it would have prompted a scene like that over the silver spoons. He was coming to terms with the irritations of travel, and even with Tibet. Near Yamdrok Tso they stopped at 'a respectable farmhouse' whose inmates proved to be 'the first Tibet people I had seen that I at all wished to be acquainted with'.

After crossing the Khamba La ('the height was trifling' – actually over 15,000 feet) they descended slowly towards the valley of the Tsang-po (or Brahmaputra) 'in which the town of Lhasa stands, distant about fifty or sixty miles'. This was the most fertile, temperate and populous belt in the whole country and, for the first time, Manning reacted with enthusiasm.

'No part of Tibet that I have seen is so pleasant . . . The valley was wide, a lively stream flowed through it, houses and villages were scattered about and, under the shelter of the mountains, on the farther side, was a large white town, pleasantly situated, and affording an agreeable prospect. The place was not destitute of trees nor of arable land, and an air of gaiety was spread over the whole and, I thought, on the faces of the people.'

They stopped to change horses in a 'clean and pleasant' yard, like that of an English inn, and were served *suchi* and good mutton 'with cheerfulness and alacrity'. At the next town they found 'a large and good ferry-boat ready to waft us over the stream'. Suddenly life was wonderful and Manning was positively bubbling. The motion of the boat so delighted him that it 'brought on a fit of European activity'. He could not sit still but clambered about from gunwale to parapet to prow, clowning and craning over the side until the skipper ordered him back to his seat. Undeterred, 'as the boat drew near shore I meditated jumping out, but was pulled back by the immense weight of my clothes and clumsiness of my boots. I was afraid of jumping short and having the laugh against me.'

That night Sid stayed up late preparing a delicacy for breakfast. Manning could hear him banging away in the kitchen till the small hours. He woke abrim with anticipation. But all that materialised was a plate of mince and a few dry biscuits. If Sid – like the attentive reader of Manning's journal – automatically steeled himself for the usual stinging outburst he was pleasantly surprised. The new Manning 'could not help laughing'.

Their last full day's march was a long one enlivened by a series of good-natured encounters. Manning even brought a smile to the face of a fractious baby by sitting himself between it and the sun's glare. Significantly – for he was definitely warming towards the Tibetans – he now travelled in the company of the Tibetan guide and together they stopped for excellent *suchi* at a little nunnery. Manning wondered whether he should turn the big prayer wheels but decided against it; 'for though I am a great conformist in certain ways, take me in another line and I am a most obstinate non-conformist, and would sooner die than swerve a little.'

They slept that night at Litong and were welcomed next day by an official from the capital. Emerging from the last town before Lhasa, the great bulk of the Potala at last hove into sight. 'It seemed close at hand but taking an eye observation upon the change of certain angles as I advanced . . . I sagaciously informed my *munshi* that it was still five or six miles off.'

This was a moment to savour. Manning was not only the first Englishman to reach Lhasa but, for nearly a century, he would be the only Englishman. Excluding the odd missionary father, he was also the first and only non-Asiatic. Where well-accredited, well-funded and well-armed missions had failed, the solitary, reluctant scholar had succeeded. Moreover, Lhasa was not just any town. It was, par excellence, the forbidden city, a place so high, so hemmed about with mountains and mystery, that it ranked in the popular imagination as a spiritual Eldorado. It was also the home of a living god. The Dalai Lama – or the Grand Lama as Manning knew him – was as fabulous a figure as Prester John, with whom he had once been identified.

But if Lhasa was all and more than the romantic traveller could desire, it was not enough to blind Manning. His euphoria of the past few days was on the wane. In Lhasa, new and numbing anxieties would take its place and colour his whole image of the city. As well as the monks thronging the streets in maroon and saffron robes, he noticed the beggars lounging in every nook and angle. The Potala, with its gilded roofs and galleries stacked above the sheer scarps of mountain and masonry, drew forth expressions of wonder. But 'if the Palace exceeded my expectations, the town fell far short of them':

'There is nothing striking, nothing pleasant in its appearance. The habitations are begrimed with smut and dirt. The avenues are full of dogs, some growling and gnawing bits of hide which lie about in profusion, and emit a charnel house smell; others limping and looking livid; others ulcerated; others starved and dying, pecked at by the ravens; some dead and preyed upon. In short, everything seems mean and gloomy, and excites the idea of something unreal. Even the mirth and laughter of the inhabitants I thought dreamy and ghostly. The dreaminess, no doubt, was in my mind, but I never could get rid of the idea; it strengthened upon me afterwards.'

The four months he would spend in Lhasa were not so much a dream as a nightmare. The news which had already plunged him into gloom was confirmation that the senior mandarin in the city was a notorious rogue who had previously held office in Canton. There he had gained a reputation as an inveterate opponent of British interests and he had probably had a hand in refusing Manning's first request to visit Peking He must have heard of Manning, of his long beard and Chinese dress; he might even recognise him; and, if he did not, it was almost certain that one of his servants would.

When detected, therefore, how should Manning act? The *munshi*, who now took charge of all negotiations and forbad Manning to utter even a syllable of Chinese during their whole stay in Lhasa, insisted that he must deny any connection with Canton or the British; he was to pass himself off as a representative of some obscure Indian caste. And above all he must suppress his British sense of dignity and conform to the customs of obeisance by making the kow-tow. Unpredictable as ever, the man who baulked at turning the odd prayer wheel had no objection to kneeling to a crooked mandarin; 'on the contrary, I was always asking when I could kneel.' But he was less happy about telling a straight lie. Hoping that his raw and wind-torn face would be sufficiently unrecognisable, he added a pair of spectacles for good measure, and duly kow-towed his way into the mandarin's august presence.

His luck was in. 'The old dog was purblind and could not see many inches beyond his nose.' There was no danger of immediate recognition. Nevertheless, suspicions were aroused and a long report was sent off to the emperor in Peking. Until a reply was received Manning and the *munshi* would be detained in Lhasa under close scrutiny. Spies hung about their lodgings, the *munshi* was frequently interrogated, and their every move was watched. It seems that Manning's identity as the suspicious doctor from Canton was guessed at; but it was never actually proved and, when accused to his face, he did manage to deny it.

This only added an uneasy conscience to a mind already tortured by anxiety. What was in that report to the emperor? And when would the reply come? He longed to know his fate but dreaded what it might be. All hope of being allowed to continue the journey to Peking must now be abandoned. It had depended on meeting with a well-disposed patron, like the general from Phari-dzong. The Canton mandarin was the exact opposite and would never countenance such a plan. His best chance was expulsion, either by way of Canton – or back the way he had come.

The alternative to expulsion was too grim to contemplate. But, for that very reason, Manning's mind, with all the perversity of genius, would contemplate little else. He tried to distract himself by composing nonsense verses and Latin puns. It did not work. Faced, for once, with the necessity of taking reality seriously, he went to the opposite extreme and magnified its horrors.

According to the panic-stricken *munshi*, the emperor's reply might well turn out to be the death sentence for both of them. The mandarin hated the British; he had tortured and executed his rivals; he would not hesitate to dispose of a couple of suspicious travellers. With all the vividness of paranoia, Manning abandoned himself to terror-stricken fantasies:

'I put myself in imagination into the situation of the prisoner accused; I suppose myself innocent; I look around; I have no resource, no refuge; instruments of torture, instruments of execution are brought by florid, high-cheeked, busy, grinning, dull-hearted men; no plea avails; no kind judge to take my part . . . This friendlessness, this nothingness of the prisoner, is what sickens me. I had rather be eaten up by a tiger than fall into such a situation and be condemned. I own I push this dread too far. Death is death; the form ought not to make so great an impression; but this superstition, to which, perhaps, my mind is by its natural texture prone, has grown upon me by reading and meditation.'

He tried to reason his way out of it, clutching at straws of good omen, blocking his ears to malicious rumour. But nothing availed. He had seen how the mandarins at Canton wielded their despotic power and the sight of it had sickened him. He could only hope that when his time came he would 'be able to submit to any fate without acting like a coward'.

The two-page paragraph in which he describes this obsession makes harrowing reading. His imagined predicament is vivid enough; but worse is the sight of Manning himself, shorn of all pretension, oblivious of wit and learning, standing face to face with a cruel death. How near he was to disintegration it is impossible to say. But he must have been wavering. This was no longer the man who bandied puns with Lamb, or stood by his silver spoons. Lhasa was changing him, irrevocably.

As his fear of the Chinese authorities grew, so he became more disposed towards their Tibetan counterparts. The Dalai Lama was only a child and Manning's first audience with him was dictated purely by courtesy and curiosity. Yet it turned out to be an equally devastating experience.

'On the 17th of December 1811, in the morning, I ascended the mountain, as they phrase it, to salute the Great Lama and make my offering.' The offering was less than he would have liked. The Bhutanese had purloined most of his broadcloth, and two china ewers, filled with artificial flowers, had been left behind at Gyantse. In their place he dug out a couple of candlesticks, property of the East India Company, polished them up, and inserted candles 'to make a good show'. He also had a few new silver coins, a good stock of Nankin tea, and two large bottles 'filled with genuine Smith's lavender water'.

With the *munshi* he rode to the Potala and climbed the four hundred steps and ladder rungs that led to the audience chamber. Outside they waited; etiquette demanded the visitor wait, and at 11,000 feet it took some time to catch one's breath.

Ushered into the divine presence, Manning kow-towed gravely, removed his hat and felt the young lama's hands being laid on his shaven head. He went through the same ceremony with the Regent, although this time distracted by an overpowering smell. One of the servants had managed to drop the Regent's bottle of genuine Smith's lavender water and 'an odiferous stream' was steadily advancing across the floor. Pretending not to notice, the guests were sat down to a bowl of *suchi*. It was the best Manning had tasted and 'I meant to have emptied the cup but it was whipped away suddenly, before I was aware of it.' He was too engrossed by the Lama's extraordinary magnetism.

'He was at that time about seven years old; had the simple and unaffected manners of a well-educated princely child. His face was, I thought, poetically and affectingly beautiful. He was of a gay and cheerful disposition; his beautiful mouth perpetually unbending into a graceful smile which illuminated his whole countenance. Sometimes, particularly when he looked at me, his smile almost approached to a gentle laugh. No doubt my grim beard and spectacles somewhat excited his risibility.'

The conversation which followed might have been marred by translation. The *munshi*, to disguise his knowledge of English, insisted on translating only into Latin. The Dalai Lama would ask a question in Tibetan, his own interpreter rendered this into Chinese, the *munshi* paraphrased into Latin and Manning quickly decoded into English. The answer was returned by the same circuitous process. Yet Manning insists that conversation was rapid and accurate; 'there was no sentiment, or shade of sentiment, which we could not exchange.' At this first interview the conversation scarcely rose above pleasantries. Yet 'I was so extremely affected . . . that I could have wept through strangeness of sensation.' Above all, it was that vision of the Lama's face which haunted him. Though 'very inexpert with the pencil' he twice tried to draw it and to capture that 'blessed smile'. He failed and, shortly after, the Dalai Lama went into retreat till the Tibetan New Year. But if any single image helped to preserve him from those 'florid, high-cheeked, grinning fiends' it was surely this other vision of a gentle humour and compassion.

In other respects the long dreary months in Lhasa were singularly unrewarding. Sid remained a trial and the *munshi* gloomy, unpredictable and unsympathetic. Manning himself suffered from severe rheumatism. He no longer relished the chance of putting on skates; indeed, he seems to have forgotten all about them. Tibetan Buddhism sporadically intrigued him, but he could obtain neither books nor a reliable mentor. That left him just his medical practice which at first thrived. Then a patient died, and the disapproval of the senior mandarin finally put paid to it altogether.

He must also have been running out of drugs but, more serious, he was short of funds. He had written to Calcutta before he reached Lhasa; the letter got lost. Now he had to start selling his effects – odd sheets, handkerchiefs, spare clothes, empty bottles and boxes, and the last of the cherry brandy, 'in short, everything I could muster up except the clothes I should probably want to use and a few keepsake trinkets'.

Poverty, though, had its advantages. Specifically, it provided a good pretext for getting rid of Sid. His wages had always seemed excessive, and the last straw came when he took Manning on a tour of the Lhasa monasteries. For some reason Manning expected this Mohammedan Chinese to know something of Tibetan Buddhism. When Sid revealed his total indifference, Manning flew into a tantrum, 'spleened', as he put it, 'by his brutish ignorance and hoggish answers'. Appropriately, Sid was next heard of having set up as a butcher.

As if to emphasise the general sense of frustration and disintegration, it is at this point – probably February 1812 – that Manning's journal abruptly stops. For his last two months in Lhasa, and for his journey out of Tibet, all we have are a few extremely cryptic notes:

'Decree arrived.
Munshi goes again to see whether anything can be
    done today.
Comes back in chains.   I anxious.
Grand Lama's kindness.

Glad when munshi goes.   Why?   Because he
   writes to me, he comes again to see me.'

And so on. At one point he suspects that he has been poisoned; at
another he sells some more empty bottles. Hopes of release
alternate with fears of 'something coming to light'. Intrigues are
hinted at, mostly concerning the poor *munshi* whose plight was
clearly far worse than his own. The attitude of the Chinese
authorities remains, at the best, ambiguous. But frequent mention
of meetings with the Dalai Lama and the Regent suggest that
Manning continued to seek consolation and support from the
Tibetans.

His departure for India seems to have been finally sanctioned at
the beginning of April. In the longest of all these notes he records
his parting with the Lama:

'April 6. I took leave of the Grand Lama with a sorrowful heart. I
said I would tell my king (Governor of Bengal) that I was well-
treated. His heart rejoices. I thank the Grand Lama and promise
that if afterwards a Lhasa man comes to Bengal it shall not be
forgotten. I take leave of Ti-mu-fu [the Regent]. Sorrowful.'

Whether he ever told the Governor-General of the Tibetan's
kindness is doubtful. He left Lhasa on April 19th, reached British
India after another brush with the Bhutanese, and passed through
Calcutta without apparently reporting to anyone. He may well
have been still resentful of the Company's indifference. Perhaps,
too, he was nursing his own wounded pride at having again failed
to reach Peking. But from now on Manning would habitually
elude society. His dotty exuberance remained; but the brilliant
and impossible scholar no longer seemed to need recognition.

He returned to Canton and in 1815 did at last get a glimpse of
Peking. This was as one of the interpreters on a grand but abortive
mission to the emperor led by Lord Amherst. His lordship had
serious doubts about taking the eccentric scholar and only agreed
to do so on condition that Manning adopt European costume.
Manning accepted provided he could keep his beard, now of
colossal proportions.

In the event the mission saw next to nothing of inland China
and, since Manning is never mentioned in the official report, it
may be assumed that his presence was little appreciated. The only
mention of him came, many years later, from Sir John Davis, one
of his fellow interpreters. Davis recalled Manning's eccentricities
with an affection that was probably not shared by the rest of the

mission. True to character, the scholar refused to take anything seriously, delighted in 'the most monstrous paradoxes' and never kept a journal.

'He did everything in his own odd and eccentric way. Being one day roused by a strange shouting I went out and discovered it was Manning who, wishing to cross the water and finding no one who would attend to him, commenced a series of howls like a dog supplemented by execrations derived from the Chinese vernacular. This led our attendant mandarins to infer that he had gone mad, and they lost no time in conveying him over the river – which was all he wanted.'

The mission over, Manning finally returned to England. Apart from two years in Italy he never travelled again. Nor, except for a book of Chinese jokes which is so rare it must have had a minute circulation, did he ever publish anything. He never attempted to edit the journal of his visit to Lhasa and its existence was not discovered till after his death. Few, indeed, knew that he had ever been there.

He was, however, recognised as an eminent sinologist, 'the first Chinese scholar in Europe', according to an obituarist. In a cottage in Kent he eventually made his home, devoid of furniture but with the best Chinese library in Britain. Here he studied and meditated, the very ideal of an oriental guru – except that his meditation was more like day-dreaming and outrageous puns were the only product of his studies. His beard, down to waist level in 1815, should now have been long enough to sit on. But again the accepted image seems to be contradicted by the facts. In a letter to Lamb of 1819 there is a suspicious mention of shaving, and in 1838 he is said to have plucked out the whole thing, now white, by the roots. This did not stop Henry Crabb Robinson in 1840 being 'charmed with Manning's personal beauty and especially with his beard'.

Later the same year he died. It was not till twenty-six years later that his journal was published and he was at last acclaimed as the first and only Englishman to have reached the Tibetan capital.

3
'A Humble and Afflicted Individual'
James Holman

Eccentric conduct is not necessarily ridiculous. If one had to chose the antithesis of the erratic and disorganised Manning, one could do worse than plump for his contemporary, James Holman. Cool, conscientious, intrepid and anything but incompetent, Holman put everyone else to shame. 'He traversed the great globe more thoroughly than any other traveller who ever existed', wrote the editor of *The Times*. 'From Marco Polo to Mungo Park', there were not even three travellers whose combined wanderings equalled those of the indomitable Holman.

Nor indeed, he might have added, had anyone else written so copiously about them. Unlike Manning, Holman took great pride in his achievements and, unlike Manning, he described them in volume upon volume of worthy prose. On a first glance at these laborious narratives one wonders whatever possessed him to write them. Scenery he ignores completely, dangers he invariably dismisses and discomforts he minimises. Instead of original observation he extracts, often without acknowledgement, great chunks of other authors' books. This apparent disregard for copyright he offsets by a scrupulous, but no less infuriating, concern for protecting the identity of those he meets. People play a large part in Holman's narrative but rarely do we discover who they are.

The most that can be said is that, to his credit, Holman freely admitted that he was not cut out to be a travel writer. Born the son of an Exeter chemist, his education had been gained in the navy. He joined it at the age of thirteen, served twelve years in the Atlantic, and retired in 1810 with the rank of lieutenant. As a preparation for the wanderings – if not the writings – that were to follow, this was no bad training. Holman took great pride in his naval career and put it to good use.

A case in point – and a good place at which to take up his story – occurred on the moonless night of 22 June 1822. Holman had just boarded a schooner as passenger and was tacking slowly down the

Thames bound for the Baltic and St Petersburg. Ever sensible in such matters, he turned in early to sleep while the going was easy. At midnight he was rudely awoken. There was a shattering crash; it felt as if the vessel had been smashed in two. In a long white nightgown he groped his way aloft. 'A large and clumsy collier had contrived to run foul of us.' The anchor cable had snapped, the figurehead was gone, and rigging strewed the deck. Moreover, the helm was deserted. Hearing the frantic commands of the captain, Holman took on himself the job of steering for safety. The captain saw the stocky white figure at the wheel and thought it was his wife. He continued to bellow commands and Holman continued to obey. Slowly the two ships inched apart. It was only afterwards, as they edged into Gravesend, that the captain correctly identified his helmsman. With a mixture of horror and amazement, like that which eventually dawns on the reader of Holman's narratives, he realised that he had just been steered to safety by a man without sight.

James Holman, the travelling phenomenon of the age, was blind. This was why he had been obliged to retire so young from the navy and why, with that mixture of courage and perversity so typical of the handicapped, he had determined to travel. It was not simply a question of rising above his affliction. He honestly believed that, for what his eyes could not see, his heightened senses of hearing, smell and touch more than compensated. But they cried out for constant and varied stimulation; for this reason he travelled. They also, he thought, gave to his travels a unique interest; and for this reason he wrote about them. In a typically long and involved passage he tried to explain:

'Deprived by the will of the Almighty of all intercourse with the visible world, the desire of locomotion has to him [the blind traveller, i.e. Holman] become a new sense, a compensating principle, which, by the succession of objects it presents, serves to fill up the deficiencies of which he would otherwise be sensible from the loss of the visual organ. It may not be easy to explain, with correctness, the nature of the sensations which are thus communicated; that numberless and interesting sensations are called forth may readily be conceived, and which, connecting themselves with ideas previously acquired . . . give rise to operations of the mind more or less pleasurable. This, however, is not all; the novelties which present themselves dependent on the habits of the people he may meet with; the accidents to which he becomes exposed, many of them rendered singularly peculiar by the peculiarity of his own circumstances; and the variety of general information he may be enabled to glean; to which may be added an almost romantic ardour to surmount difficulties; all conspire to throw an interest, sometimes nearly magical, over his wanderings.'

It is important to remember that he had not been blind from birth. Until the age of twenty-five his sight had been normal. How he lost it is not clear, but it was the result of an illness (scurvy?) rather than an accident. At first he had high hopes of recovery. Invalided out of the navy he went to Edinburgh to study – and be studied – at the medical school. It was two years before he accepted his fate and retired on half pay to a grace and favour appointment at Windsor. There the horror of his situation came home to him. Barely thirty, naturally active, and inordinately curious, he was consigned to a long and useless retirement. For five years he stuck it out. Then in 1819, to the consternation of his friends, he set off for Dover. He crossed to Calais on his thirty-third birthday and headed south.

This first tour lasted three years. He regretted not a day of it. He relied entirely on public transport, he spoke no foreign language, and he travelled alone without even a servant. Yet neither wars, earthquakes, accidents, shipwrecks nor hijackings slowed his steady progress. One by one he relentlessly notched up the sights and cities of western Europe. In Marseilles he caused alarm by leaping from one of the bathing boats and swimming straight for Africa; he reckoned that the shouts of fellow bathers would always tell him which way lay the shore. In Rome he climbed inside the dome of St Peter's and was all for getting on the roof to scale the lightning conductor. The blind, he protested, were immune to vertigo. He proved his point when on an excursion up Vesuvius he tiptoed round the crater on stepping stones. The end of his stick was charred and his shoes filled with volcanic ash; but this was all part of the experience.

Returning home in 1821 he had barely six months to recover and write his first narrative before boarding that schooner for the Baltic. His plan now was to visit the Russian empire. That, at least, was what he told his friends. Holman was a sensitive soul; he wished neither to invite ridicule nor to cause alarm. But, as he later confessed, his real motive, 'should circumstances prove propitious', was nothing less than that of 'making a circuit of the whole world'.

After forty-eight hours in Gravesend docks, the schooner put back to sea. The wind was favourable and the captain so delighted by his new helmsman that he gave him another spell of duty. On July 2nd they landed at Elsinore but stopped only long enough to breakfast. Holman pleaded for a chance to explore the palace and seek out Ophelia's watery grave. But time was short; and besides, if ever an author was justified in penning a description of something he had not seen, it was Holman. That night they anchored off Copenhagen. Their next landing, a week later, was at Cronstadt, the port for St Petersburg.

Here the inevitable customs delays afforded a chance of spending a day with 'the Revd Mr B—, an English clergyman resident at this place'. Significantly Mr B— had heard of Holman, 'through the medium of the press'; he was still within the sphere of his own considerable celebrity and not without friends. One such awaited him at the end of a droshka ride through the imperial capital, none other than 'my old and particular friend, Mr C—'.

Mr C— (or Mr C–l–b–k–, as Holman incautiously reveals in the excitement of the rencontre) was one of the main incentives for coming to St Petersburg. The two men had originally met on the other side of the Atlantic when Holman was still in the navy. C— was evidently an American citizen. But it was at Naples, on his first journey as a blind traveller, that Holman rediscovered his friend. Immediately the two men got on famously. Both had a passion for travel, both were far from wealthy, and both enjoyed a joke at the other's expense. Nor was this all. For whilst Holman had become blind, poor C— had lost his hearing. These shared afflictions caused each of them endless delight and, as they pooled their resources and travelled on together, the blind man and the deaf met with a warmer reception than ever. Communications between the two were obviously difficult but this was more than offset by the advantages derived in dealing with the outside world. C— had acquired a tireless negotiator, Holman a reliable pilot and informant. And each had acquired a friend whose patience and resourcefulness matched his own. For a thousand miles, from Naples to Amsterdam, they shared the joys and tribulations of the road. In Rome C— arranged for a male model to range himself amongst the Vatican sculptures. Holman, sampling their form by touch as was his custom, duly moved from a cold marble torso to a soft hairy knee; he was suitably discomfited. And what a moving sight they must have made standing spellbound before the great clock of Strasbourg as C— tried to imagine its chimes whilst Holman conjured up its workings.

Holman, no doubt, had high hopes of persuading C— to take the road once again. He moved into C—'s lodgings and during the six months that he devoted to the sights and social doings of St Petersburg, C— was his constant cicerone. Together they enquired minutely into the academies, archives, orphanages and oratories. They explored the markets and they rambled through the palaces and galleries. In the days before Baedeker there was no more insatiable tourist than the blind Holman and no more eager informant than the deaf C—. When the winter season got under way they turned their attention to an endless succession of 'entertainments' – theatres, balls, concerts and dinners. Holman, particularly, relished the chance to mingle with the mighty. He lived in a world of atmospheres and there was none more eloquent or comforting than the whisper of silks and the scent of cigars. He also regarded himself as something of a ladies' man. 'To assert that there are no handsome women in Russia is a libel scarce to be credited,' he declared, 'at all events, the exceptions are most numerous.' But how could he tell?

'My power of discriminating female beauty has so often been called in question and I have so frequently been told that it matters not to me whether a woman be handsome or not, that a few words in explanation may not be *mal à-propos*. When introduced to a lady, if I find her conversation sensible and refined and her tone of voice agreeable, I immediately assume that other qualities more or less harmonise and that her personal attractions may also be pleasing. Imagination now commences and finds no difficulty in heightening the picture so as to paint her even as beautiful. It is true that I am liable to error in forming opinions from such data. But if, in addition, opportunity is afforded me of feeling the hand and touching, ever so lightly, the features of the face, I fancy that I can, from their softness, delicacy or contour, arrive at conclusions so certain that I am vain enough to imagine that they have not often proved erroneous.'

There were advantages in being blind. People, and particularly women, were more inclined to trust and confide in you. A polite request to take a lady's hand or feel her complexion was rarely refused and often appreciated. On the first tour a succession of doting landladies and hostesses had eased his progress, and if an inn was overcrowded, his was invariably the privilege of sharing a room with the ladies. There is nothing to suggest that Holman abused this position. Off Genoa he had spent three days and three nights alone in the cabin of their grounded vessel with an enticing but distraught signorina. He took much pleasure in comforting her but apparently remained the perfect gentleman.

In all Holman filled eight chapters with the life and times of St Petersburg. It was a measure of his attachment to the city. Leaving meant foregoing the chance of another game of bowls at the prestigious English Club. (He claimed to play as good a game as the sighted.) It meant saying goodbye to dear C— who could not be persuaded to accompany him. And it meant placing himself in the uncertain care of the Russian authorities. The journey to Moscow was straightforward enough; he arrived there by public sledge in March 1823. But to obtain the permissions and to make the necessary arrangements for continuing east he had now to declare his plans.

'When my intention [of heading into Siberia] first began to transpire at Moscow, everyone made it his business to demonstrate the madness and absurdity of attempting so dangerous, uninteresting and disagreeable a journey in a country where, as respecting myself, nothing was to be either seen or heard. [Needless to say, Holman spoke no Russian.] In short the name of Siberia seemed connected in their minds only with horror. Not a stranger to whom I was casually introduced, but made it the first object of his conversation to fish into my plans and endeavour to dissuade me from their prosecution. It was kindly meant but my determination was inflexible.'

Of all those who tried to dissuade him none carried more weight than the British traveller, Captain John Dundas Cochrane. Cochrane arrived in Moscow in May and Holman was still there to greet him. Indeed he had been waiting for him. For Cochrane knew the ropes. He was coming not from England but from Siberia by the very route which Holman hoped to follow.

It is significant that Holman makes no attempt to conceal Cochrane's identity with an initial. On the contrary, he wanted his readers to know all about the captain. Here was another ex-naval officer and another notable eccentric. But there the similarity stopped; never were the extremes of eccentricity better exemplified. Cochrane was the grandson of an earl whose family can boast more admirals than any in the kingdom. In 1805 he found himself in the undignified position of being without a ship. He therefore invited the Admiralty to send him in the footsteps of Mungo Park to explore the River Niger. The Admiralty declined and Cochrane struck out on his own. After a few trial runs in Europe he embarked on an ambitious plan to be the first man to walk round the world. His chosen route was the northern hemisphere – Europe, Russia, Siberia, Alaska, Canada. This, he thought, would neatly complement, if not upstage, Captain Parry's attempt to do the same thing by sea.

No one doubted the captain's prowess as a walker. He had once done ninety-six non-stop miles in thirty-two hours and was as much 'the pedestrian traveller' as Holman was 'the blind traveller'. But there was too much of the showman about Cochrane. He lacked that 'inflexible determination' of Holman's and his resolve crumbled. He was now on his way home via Moscow.

For one thing he had discovered that Siberia was no place for pedestrians, especially in mid winter. Reluctantly he had compromised and travelled by sledge. In this way he did reach Kamchatka, the eastern extremity of Siberia. But alas for Alaska. In Kamchatka he had fallen madly in love with the fifteen-year-old daughter of an Indian Chief. Forgetful of his grand design, he married her and was now escorting his young bride back to England.

The young lady had never before strayed from her native Kamchatka and when Holman was introduced to her he thought it only right she should see the sights of Moscow. He took her to the theatre ('we did not notice that expression of astonishment which we had anticipated') and he took her on his fourth tour of the Kremlin ('she appeared pleased with what she saw but not at all surprised'). Diminutive and doe-eyed, she was by all accounts a great beauty but it was a pity that her natural diffidence prevented a true friendship.

Diffidence was not one of the Captain's failings. Cochrane thought that Holman must be out of his mind to wish to cross Siberia, and told him so. Did he, for instance, have permission from the Minister of the Interior for his journey? He did not; nor, on enquiring through the normal channels, did it appear that he needed it. Then, as now, there were double standards about the freedom of travellers within the Russian dominions. Holman would soon discover this to his cost. But equally it appears that Cochrane was trying to raise every possible objection.

Reluctantly the Captain agreed to sell Holman his pavoshka, a springless four-wheeled cart, and with it came his dour Tartar postilion. But that was not the end of the matter. He still thought Holman was crazy and he returned to the attack with a cloying mixture of sympathy and sarcasm in his published narrative. No one should question the blind man's courage, wrote Cochrane, but why on earth did he insist on going to Siberia. Of course, 'he may go there as well as anywhere else, for he will see just as much, but there is so little to be seen by those who even have the use of their eyes that I cannot divine what interest he can have to attempt it.' How could he hope to learn anything useful when he could not understand a word of the language and when his only informants were likely to be exiled criminals? And how was he proposing to get his notes home without their being censored?

Holman took great pride in the accuracy of his observations and resented this questioning bitterly. He replied through the press and in his own narrative. By then he had read Cochrane's account and could not, for the life of him, understand why the captain had visited Siberia. If there was so little to see then surely the prospects for the blind were as good as for the sighted. And as for the danger of his notes being censored, he was happy to report that he had developed a method of note-taking 'which might not have entered into the captain's contemplation – that of depositing them in a portable and invisible form within the cavity of my cranium'.

Holman's memory was a phenomenon in its own right. With unerring precision he could recall not just people and places, but dimensions, dates and distances. Blindness had taught him to be methodical. When preparing to leave Moscow he shut himself away for several hours to concentrate on packing. Every item had its precise place and should anything be tampered with he knew about it immediately. His bankers, Messrs G— and H— (why on earth conceal the name of one's bankers?), had kindly supplied him with an ample stock of small change. This had to be sorted into twenty-, forty- and eighty-copeck pieces, each carefully stowed in separate bags. Then there was his medical chest, clothing and, of course, supplies for the journey.

'I was provided with tea and sugar for the whole journey; six bottles of brandy and as many of French wine. And I always took care to lay in at each town sufficient bread and meat to serve until our arrival at the next; and thus, having also with me a teapot, cups etc., I was quite independent of the accidental and inadequate entertainment the post-houses could furnish, with the exception of hot water.'

On 12 June 1823 he was ready. He saw off the Cochranes, who were just leaving for St Petersburg, returned to his lodgings and climbed into the pavoshka. The postilion mounted, a host of acquaintances waved him off, and the pavoshka jolted off into the forest.

'My situation was now one of extreme novelty, and my feelings corresponded with its novelty. I was engaged under circumstances of unusual occurrence in a solitary journey of several thousand miles through a country perhaps the wildest on the face of the earth and whose inhabitants were scarcely yet accounted within the pale of civilisation, with no other attendant than a rude Tartar postilion to whose language my ear was wholly unaccustomed. And yet I was supported by a feeling of happy confidence with a calm resignation to all the inconveniences and risks of my arduous undertaking.'

There was no public transport east of Moscow, but for the equivalent of £9 Holman had taken out a post licence. This theoretically entitled him to fresh horses for his pavoshka all the way from Moscow to Irkutsk, a distance of over three thousand five hundred miles. It was, of course, too good to be true and his early preoccupations were largely those of commandeering the promised horses or negotiating for others. The rude postilion proved of little help. Instead, Holman fell back on the letters of introduction which he had been assiduously collecting ever since he landed at Cronstadt. Carefully memorised and filed, these now numbered several hundred and included practically every senior official and foreigner in the empire. Sometimes he would draw a blank; his prospective host would be absent. More often he would be met with incredulity; the blind Englishman and his sour Tartar would be taken for imposters, practical jokers or itinerant actors. Then the letter of introduction would be produced. Apologies followed and the traveller was soon sitting down to a sumptuous dinner with the prospect of a good night's sleep and fresh horses in the morning. After a night or two on the road, or on a bench in a posting station, the luxuries of linen and plate were duly appreciated. Even more valuable, in the dark and silent world that was Holman's, was the opportunity of conversation. Few spoke English but on his first tour Holman had picked up some French. This proved invaluable, and if the naturally curious traveller appeared bent on systematic interrogations it was hardly surprising; these chance meetings were his only link with reality.

Such, then, was the pattern of his journey. The roads were appalling, either deep in mud or composed of undressed tree trunks. Had the pavoshka had springs they would not have lasted a day; even the axles broke with depressing regularity. As a relief from the incessant jolting Holman sometimes walked or ran. A light rope tied round his waist and attached to the back of the cart ensured that he did not get left behind.

On July 15th, a month after leaving Moscow, he crossed the Urals and entered Asia.

'My heart bounded with joy that I had accomplished so considerable a part of my journey and was entering, as it were, upon a new world, a world of strangers, with Providence only as my guide. I had now succeeded in what had been for many years one of the most ardent objects of my wishes but which I had little expectation of realising – a desire of visiting the fourth quarter of the globe. The satisfaction I felt is indescribable.'

Drunk with the raw sensation of travel, he felt that some supernatural power was carrying him onwards. Anything was possible. Another month jolted by. He crossed the river Irtysh on a raft and reached Tobolsk, the capital of Western Siberia.

Tobolsk proved ill-endowed with notable buildings. Holman had exhausted its sight-seeing potential in a couple of days. Its society, too, was limited. The men outnumbered the ladies by four to one and their principal recreations were cards and billiards, neither of which fell within his range of accomplishments. He was as hospitably received and entertained as ever; but something was wrong. He detected a note of reserve in the Governor-General and an extraordinary insensitivity in some of his colleagues.

In particular they seemed intent on quizzing him about his previous journeys. When Holman mentioned having visited the island of St Helena, the Governor of Tobolsk improbably exclaimed that he had a picture of the place and leapt up to fetch it. It was quite extraordinary how easily people could forget that he was blind. Nor was this the first time it had happened. 'Occasionally they have only had their recollection recalled by some unexpected movement of my hand overthrowing what they offered as, for instance, a cup of tea.' Others, apparently mistaking his deprivation, would persistently shout at him as if he were deaf or insist on his squeezing everything 'as if I were about to ascertain the condition of a bird or beast'. In fact his hearing was excellent and his sense of touch 'most delicate'. 'All that I require is to pass the hand lightly over a body and then the result is both pleasing and satisfactory.'

While the Governor was gone for his painting of St Helena, Holman grew very curious about a heavy breathing sound that was filling the room. It came from knee level and sounded vaguely feral. Could it be, he enquired, that he was in the presence of 'some non-descript Siberian animal'?

'Unfortunately it was one of the principal counsellors of Tobolsk who had a peculiar obstruction in his nasal organs which produced the singular wheezing noise – besides the gentleman was of very diminutive stature so that his head was not much above the level of a good-sized Newfoundland dog . . . This proves how cautious we ought to be in *speaking in the dark*.'

The rare italics suggest that this little anecdote had its purpose. In view of what lay ahead it seems certain that Holman was in fact on trial – and he knew it. The Governor of Tobolsk, with his picture of St Helena, was trying to find out whether this solitary traveller with his endless questions was in fact as blind as he appeared. Holman's little mistake about the wheezing counsellor was therefore an attempt to convince the assembled company that he was, if anything, even blinder.

From Tobolsk the road ran eastwards along the bank of the Irtysh and then plunged into the foggy marshes of the Barabinski steppe. Here the water was so poisoned by a species of hemlock that any animal drinking from it immediately died. The atmosphere was no better, being loaded with malaria (or 'miasmatic impregnations'), typhus and other fevers, one of which produced boils of gigantic size and fatal consequence. The marshes were also the breeding ground of the notorious Siberian mosquito, which could descend on the traveller in such numbers that he died of suffocation. Holman took the accepted precaution of donning a gauze outfit, like a bee-keeper's, and was further helped by incessant rain which dampened down both the insects and the impregnations. 'I experienced, however, quite sufficient to convince me that the details of other travellers with respect to this country are by no means fabulous.'

The next big river was the Ob and the next big town Tomsk. Tomsk is on the same longitude as Calcutta. He was already two thousand miles from Moscow and still going strong. His health was excellent and he was far from bored. There was, he admitted, little about Siberia to distract the mind. But he was happy enough immersed in his own thoughts and took a positive delight in just feeling the miles slip by.

Tomsk was notable for the Vice-Governor's two 'very amiable' daughters, its otherwise vile accommodations, and Holman's first attempt at doctoring. As luck would have it his patient, the gloomy postilion, was experiencing opthalmic problems. This was an area of medicine in which Holman felt peculiarly qualified. He duly prescribed and the man's severely inflamed eyes obligingly responded. They left Tomsk on September 3rd and reached Krasnoyarsk a week later. A long caravan carrying brick tea from China served as a reminder that they were nearer Peking than Moscow. In fact Irkutsk, the next port of call, was only sixty miles from what was then the Chinese frontier and is now that of Outer Mongolia. Holman arrived there on September 18th and, after three months on the road since Moscow, resolved on a prolonged stay.

Irkutsk was the capital of Eastern Siberia and the last outpost of civilisation before the Bering Straits and the Pacific. Here his post licence expired. Permissions and carriage for the last leg on Russian territory would have to be negotiated and supplies organised. He understood that the journey onwards would be much easier if he waited for the snows of winter and travelled by sledge. He hoped also to make a brief excursion to the Chinese frontier and this too would be a simpler affair if he could wait till the waters of Lake Baikal had frozen over.

He therefore moved into lodgings and settled down to explore the society of the town. In this he was pleasantly surprised. 'It would scarcely be credited in Europe that the state of society in this distant part of the world could be so luxurious and polished.' Invitations to dinners, picnics, fishing parties and balls poured in. Something of the frontier spirit clung to Irkutsk. It was livelier than Tomsk or Tobolsk and retained a great respect for the traveller and the pioneer. The blind Englishman became the hero of the hour and for the first two months all doors were open to him. In particular there was the mysterious Mrs B—, the widow of a Russian officer and, surprisingly, an Englishwoman. Holman took a special delight in the company of 'my fair countrywoman' and in describing her circumstances hints at an almost intimate relationship. Wealthy, respected, in her mid-thirties and a great beauty, she remained loyal to her husband's memory but was clearly delighted by Holman's attentions.

There was also the Governor of Irkutsk, whose family partially adopted Holman, and above all, the Governor-General of the province. Holman had never enjoyed such a close relationship with a high Imperial official. They walked together arm in arm, rode through the town and toured the surrounding districts. He seemed 'to combine the sincerity of an Englishman and the politeness of a Frenchman with the refined hospitality of a Russian'. Emboldened by all this, Holman resolved to divulge, 'what I had done to no other person before', his plan to continue right round the world. The Governor-General was not enthusiastic. He tried hard to dissuade him and then insisted that though Holman might continue on to Kamchatka he would need special permission from the Emperor to embark from any of the Russian Pacific ports. Reluctantly he did agree to send off the necessary letter of application; but so much opposition from a man who seemed so friendly was a bad omen.

Meanwhile the social season wore on and the temperature started to fall. On October 22nd there were twelve degrees of frost and the first snow fell. Holman and the Governor-General fortified themselves with a visit to the local distillery. A month later the mercury was down to minus thirteen degrees Fahrenheit, on December 7th it touched minus thirty-five and a few days later it froze solid at the bottom of the thermometer. It stayed there. Holman continued to go his rounds on foot in preference to a sledge but was 'obliged frequently to rub my nose and cheeks to prevent them from freezing, a precaution I found necessary in consequence of having had one cheek frost bitten a few days before'.

Christmas Day – which was not of course the Russian Christmas – he spent with the fair Mrs B—. By New Year Lake Baikal was reported frozen over and the short cut to the Chinese frontier was therefore open. Holman's plan was to make his excursion coincide with the Chinese New Year, due sometime in February. It was not to be. On January 2nd the Governor-General sat him down after dinner and communicated the orders just received from St Petersburg. Far from sanctioning his sailing from one of the Pacific ports, the Emperor Alexander was opposed to his proceeding any further than Irkutsk; indeed he was distressed to learn that Holman had got that far without an attendant. He had therefore sent a lieutenant of the corps of feld-jagers to accompany him on his return journey.

Ostensibly the Emperor's only concern was the comfort and safety of the blind Englishman. But Holman already sensed that this was not the whole story. The Governor-General was clearly embarrassed and trying to hold something back. Mysteriously he insisted that Holman should keep the whole matter a secret. And why should the officer sent be from the feld-jagers which was the Tsarist equivalent of the KGB? A poor blindman scarcely deserved such an exalted guide-dog.

Holman slipped away from the Governor-General's as quickly as he decently could. 'The intelligence I had received acted almost as an electric shock upon me.' He was badly shaken and bitterly disappointed. Self-pity he had long ago rejected but those waves of isolation and helplessness which stalk the blind all but engulfed him. He concentrated his mind on the memory of maps once seen. If he must turn back, surely he could take a different route. The Caspian and the Black Sea perhaps, and then Constantinople and a long ramble through Greece and the Balkans.

Before the night was out he had made his plan and written to his bankers to inform them. A week of festivities for the Russian Christmas then slipped by pleasantly enough. But soon the

Governor-General was again pressing for his departure; it would be 'indelicate' not quickly to accept such a generous offer as the Emperor had made. Holman protested that he had first to visit the Chinese frontier. But this, he was told, was now out of the question. Nor could he choose his route back across Russia. His only choice was between being escorted to the Prussian or the Austrian frontiers.

There was a certain relief in knowing the true nature of his circumstances. He felt, if anything, rather elated by these new revelations. Far from being treated as an object of pity, he was evidently under heavy suspicion – a state prisoner, no less, ordered out of the country under escort. It was preposterous, of course, but it put the frustration of his plans in a much more interesting, even heroic, light. He immediately wrote an official complaint to the British Ambassador and made it clear to all that he was innocent of any crime and was submitting under protest. The temptation to get his own back by attacking the arbitrary nature of Tsarist rule he resisted. He had never yet betrayed the hospitality of his Russian hosts and he had no intention of doing so now when it would obviously reflect on his innocence. But what lay behind the incident remained a mystery. All Holman could adduce was that someone had wilfully misrepresented to the Emperor either the purpose of his journey or his behaviour. Could it, one wonders, have been Cochrane? And if not, who else had something against the blind traveller?

On January 18th, with the feld-jager at his side, Holman set off back to Moscow. The old pavoshka had been hastily exchanged for a sledge and the goodbyes quickly said. There remained only Mrs B— at whose house on the Angara river Holman made his final call. Mrs B— was suitably distraught and so, to judge by the little verse unexpectedly inserted in his narrative, was Holman.

The stranger is gone – Oh, he will not forget,
When at home he shall talk of the toil he has known,
To tell with a sigh what endearments he met,
As he strayed on the banks of Angara alone.

The memories grew proportionately fonder as the journey back across Russia unfolded. Holman expected that opportunities of mingling in society would now be severely restricted by his companion. But he reckoned without the man's obsession with speed; he seemed intent on a new trans-Siberian sledging record. He stopped for food, for fresh horses, and to beat the driver. Otherwise, night or day, blizzard or no blizzard, they ploughed on.

Collisions, somersaults and snowdrifts failed to convince him of the dangers, and only when Holman was clearly ill would he reluctantly consent to a day's rest. Admittedly Holman was not exactly being hustled through a traveller's paradise. The forests and steppes and tundra, dreary enough in the summer, were now shrouded in several feet of snow with their scant population hibernating. The temperature was stuck at about minus fifty degrees Fahrenheit and even when snow was not actually falling, the arctic winds whipped up what lay on the ground and created their own 'white-out' conditions.

All in all a more challenging situation for the aspiring travel writer it would be hard to construct. As he hurtled across the four thousand miles of wintry monotony, seeing nothing, conversing with nobody, despondent, exhausted and indescribably cold, Holman admitted that this had to be the very negation of travel. The only concession which he had won from his captor was a minor alteration to their route; from Tomsk they would take a more southerly line to Tobolsk by way of Omsk. This proved even less exciting than it sounds for Omsk had just been burnt down. However, amidst the ruins, Holman met some acquaintances from Tobolsk who managed briefly to whisk him away from the feld-jager.

They took him to visit an encampment of 'Kirghiz' (actually Kazakh) nomads just outside the town. It was his last little adventure in Siberia and he made the most of it. After minutely examining everything in their tents he enquired whether it might be in order for him to 'salute' the ladies. The interpreter raised no objections and Holman 'determined to venture upon the experiment'.

'I commenced with the older one, paving the way by putting a piece of money into her hand. She took the whole very kindly, which encouraged me to move to the next in years and dignity, who was also by no means displeased on the occasion. The young woman, however, whom I understood was very pretty and very reserved, hung down her head with at least the affectation of modesty, and it was only with some difficulty that I succeeded in securing a half stolen kiss.'

Few instances could better testify to the unique advantages enjoyed by the blind. What other traveller could claim to have kissed a Kirghiz maiden?

In spite of this diversion, and a night spent at Omsk, Holman and the feld-jager covered the one thousand five hundred miles from Tomsk to Ekaterinberg (now Sverdlovsk) in an amazing nine days. Against the cold, which still kept the mercury frozen in the thermometers, he was well prepared; his feet were 'encased in two pairs of woollen stockings with two pairs of fur boots, the outer ones of leather lined with fur and having thick soles to them, the inner ones made of the skin of the wild goat. The body, independent of my ordinary clothing, was covered over with a thickly wadded great-coat, over which I wore an immense shube, made of the skins of wolves, while the head was protected by a wadded cap.' Yet in the open sledge he was still in danger of frostbite – their driver lost a big toe in this way – and still too cold to sleep. Travelling day and night for days on end, it was sheer exhaustion that was undermining his rugged constitution. He desperately needed rest, something the feld-jager would not hear of. Even when they reached Moscow in late February the man was all for pushing on immediately. Holman put his foot down.

A doctor was called and duly certified him as unfit to be moved. He was therefore installed in a hotel and given three days to recuperate under the bespectacled gaze of a sinister plain-clothes man. The fiction that he was simply being attended for his own good was wearing thin. Moscow was rife with rumours of his arrest and he was forbidden to leave the hotel or even to communicate with his friends. Holman thought he might get round this by issuing an unaddressed circular. Accordingly, when his guard was asleep, he crept out of bed, dug out his 'writing machine' (something called the Via Nocto Polygraph) and drew up a suitable notice.

CIRCULAR

The prisoner Holman begs leave to acquaint his friends in Moscow that he has just arrived from Siberia under charge of a feld-jager. As his keeper does not allow him to visit his friends, he begs to inform them that he may be seen at the Hôtel de l'Europe for three days only. . .

The notice was smuggled out by one of his bankers and quickly circulated. Although none of his Russian acquaintances dared incur official displeasure, a few English friends called at the hotel and were admitted. But even then the plain-clothes man was in constant attendance and, because he knew no English, all conversation had to be conducted in Holman's faltering French. When the three days were up Holman, still sick, was asked, then ordered, to leave with the feld-jager. He now realised that his official complaint must never have reached the British Ambassador in St Petersburg. In Moscow there was not even a British consul. Any hopes of redress thus faded. With a final breathless outburst of indignation he resigned himself to extradition.

'How ridiculous it must appear that the government of the mighty Russian Empire should make the residence of a day or two longer in its territories of a single humble and afflicted individual like myself an object of such immense importance as to induce them to hurry himself away at the risk of his life; an individual and subject of a friendly nation from which they had accepted and are still accepting all the rights of hospitality, against whom no offence either political or moral has been proved – or even so much as brought to the threshold of accusation – and whom they (hypocritically indeed) professed to consider not as a prisoner but as a gentleman travelling for his own gratification; and yet were cruel enough to compel him, contrary to his inclinations, to an incessant journey of nearly five thousand miles, at this inclement season, through the wildest country in the world, extending over him the strictest and most jealous surveillance, and denying from him the privilege of seeing a friend in private or of even addressing a countryman in his native language.'

On March 5th, six days after leaving Moscow, he was deposited in Cracow in Poland, a free citizen once again. At first he felt simply indifferent. For one so methodical and meticulous the unsettling effect of being suddenly whisked half across the world was as injurious to his well-being as the physical exhaustion. His passport was out of order, his financial arrangements were uncertain and, for the Austrian Empire, he had none of those precious letters of introduction. It was a month before he felt able to proceed and even then he never quite recaptured his old verve for exploring the sights. Travelling by way of Vienna, Dresden, Berlin and Hamburg, he sailed for home, landing at Hull on 20 June 1824.

'I need scarcely express the rapturous feeling with which I once more hailed my native land, having learnt during my absence more highly to appreciate its vast superiority over the extensive regions I had been traversing. Happy England, land of liberty, of virtue, and of beauty; chief nurse of science, munificent patroness of the arts; boundless in commerce and opulence; matchless in arms; and super-eminent over every other country in national glory.'

In the wake of such sentiments he received a coveted permission to dedicate the account of his journey to the king, George IV. The book appeared in 1825 and quickly ran through four editions. 'We have seldom met with any work so replete with interesting information,' commented the *Observer*, and another reviewer, considering this and the previous narrative together, reckoned 'these works of Lieutenant Holman the most extraordinary that have ever appeared in any age or country'. Holman was famous. He was now back at Windsor as a pensioner of the Crown, somewhat better off financially than he had been six years before but no more resigned to his fate. He still considered that the only antidote to blindness was the sort of relentless sensory bombardment which travel provided and he still nursed his great ambition – 'to make a circuit of the whole world'.

Happily he was not to be disappointed. In 1827 HMS *Eden* was despatched to the west coast of Africa to found an anti-slavery settlement on the island of Fernando Po in the Bight of Biafra. Her captain invited Holman to sail with him and, on the grounds that a warmer climate would be good for his general health, Holman obtained leave from the grace and favour post at Windsor. Convalescence in an area popularly known as the White Man's Grave might appear an odd choice. But Holman believed that it was not the climate that was unhealthy but the diet and lifestyle of those who were sent there. Exercise and abstinence should prove powerful antidotes and, during a year in which more than half his shipmates died, he proved his point. His health was excellent and when the occasional twinge of fever did betray itself he had his own sensible remedy: 'I took calomel, abstained from all food, taking only liquids, keeping myself quiet, and occupying the mind with amusing thoughts.'

His one-volume account of his stay on Fernando Po deserves more attention than it has received. There can be few more complete or fascinating insights into the business of founding a settlement from scratch. The first landfall, the first contacts with an extremely primitive people, surveying the island (one of the rivers was named the Holman), and laying out the fort (called Clarence with suburbs Bushy Park, Longfields, Paradise and Newlands) are all described with a guileless pride. Holman not only acted as the self-appointed chronicler of the expedition but himself played a leading role, being one of the first to explore the interior and the first to sample monkey stew. To the naked inhabitants his blindness must have come as welcome evidence that the white newcomers were indeed members of the human race and subject to the same afflictions as themselves. His fellow settlers remained suspicious and vigilant but Holman would happily give his arm to anyone who would willingly take it. Such confidence was generously repaid.

'Soon after landing this morning I fell in with a party of natives with whom I shook hands as usual. But a young female, perceiving that I did not immediately recognise her as an old acquaintance, placed my hand on her bosom. Her relatives and countrymen all laughed heartily and appeared to enjoy my astonishment much. If, however, any of us had ventured upon such a liberty of our own accord, the men would have been highly indignant for they are extremely jealous of their women.'

On Christmas Day 1827 formal possession of Clarence was taken with a long proclamation, three cheers, God Save the King and a royal salute from the *Eden*. By April the barracks were up and the first houses ready. But it was the hospital that was proving the best patronised structure. Holman was one of only a handful who were still fit for duty. The sick needed to be evacuated and more men to be brought in. It was decided to send the *Eden* back to Sierra Leone and Holman went with her. He had exhausted the novelties of Fernando Po.

His plans were now flexible. He considered a tour of Sierra Leone and perhaps, like Cochrane, fancied his chances of solving the mystery that still surrounded the fate of the great Mungo Park. Then, off Ascension Island, the *Eden* fell in with a Dutch vessel bound for Rio de Janeiro. It was an opportunity which the cautious and methodical Holman of a few years back would scarcely have noticed. Now, a seasoned and adventurous traveller but forty-two years old and still with three-quarters of the globe to explore, he did not hesitate. A decision which would once have had him agonising for pages was reached, without comment, in a single sentence. He sailed for Brazil.

Thus began the extraordinary odyssey of random voyages which, over the next four years, would at last take him round the world. The story is told in four packed volumes, each of more than five hundred pages. It lacks the cohesion and the freshness of the Siberian journey; by the end one feels that even Holman's appetite for novelty was nearing satiety. But it is indeed a unique tour de force.

From Brazil he visited the Cape Province, Zanzibar, Mauritius, Ceylon, Madras, Calcutta, Canton, Tasmania, New South Wales, New Zealand and Brazil again before sailing back up the Thames. These long and often boring voyages were, however, only the links in a series of overland excursions of far more interest and challenge. From Rio he rode high into the interior to inspect the mining country on the edge of the Mato Grosso; and from

Capetown he trekked five hundred miles round the coast. Here, riding a gigantic horse, he had three of his worst falls and, but for his hard black beaver hat, would have fractured his skull. Zanzibar, Ceylon and Tasmania he crossed on foot and in New South Wales he explored the coastal ranges south of Sydney. In Canton he tried opium, in South Africa he got lost in a cloud of locusts, and in Ceylon, with a little help from his friends, he shot elephant and alligator.

As usual he travelled alone and on 'extremely limited pecuniary means', relying on 'Divine protection and on the sympathies of mankind to the claims of persons circumstanced as I am'. Happily 'I was not disappointed'. His story says as much for his fellow men as for himself. There was not a single instance of his having been cheated, let alone robbed. The roughest handling he had ever experienced was still that meted out by the Tsar and his feldjager.

If he had one real regret it was not that he could not see the wonders of nature but that he was unable to describe them adequately. In a poignant out-pouring he expressed a frustration which must be familiar to all blind people:

'On the summit of the precipice and in the deep green woods emotions as palpable and as true have agitated me as if I were surveying them with the blessing of sight. There was an intelligence in the winds of the hills and in the solemn stillness of the buried foliage that could not be mistaken. It entered into my heart and I could have wept, not that I did not see, but that I could not portray all I felt.'

In the 1840s he made one final journey – to the eastern Mediterranean – but the narrative of it was never given for publication. He died in London in 1857.

4
'A White Man from Yorkshire'
Charles Waterton

In a long introduction to his *Essays on Natural History*, Charles Waterton decided to bow to the curiosity of the public and supply an autobiographical sketch. He understood that readers also like to have a portrait of the author. Unfortunately, in this respect he could not oblige. He had a deep-seated repugnance to sitting for an artist. Instead, he would provide a brief, and brutal, pen portrait.

'I was born at Walton Hall, near Wakefield, in the county of York some five and fifty years ago: this tells me that I am no chicken; but . . . in fact I feel as though I were not more than thirty years old. I am quite free from all rheumatic pains, and am so supple in the joints that I can climb a tree with the utmost facility . . . I stand six feet high, all but half an inch. On looking at myself in the mirror I can see at once that my face is anything but comely. Continual exposure to the sun and the rains of the tropics has furrowed it in places and given it a tint which neither Rowland's Kalydor, nor all the cosmetics on Belinda's toilette, would ever be able to remove.'

His hair, once 'a shade betwixt black and brown' now looked as if it had 'passed the night exposed to a November hoar-frost'. And it was cut unfashionably short, crew-cut in fact. Above the waist his physique was unremarkable; but his legs, he thought, evidenced 'vast muscular power', the product of half a century of tree climbing. 'Were I exhibited for show at a horse fair, some learned jockey would explain "he is half Rosinante, half Bucephalus".'

With a typically scrupulous regard for the truth, he admitted that he had in fact once sat for his portrait. The artist was Charles Peale of Philadelphia (the father, incidentally, of Raphael, Rembrandt, Rubens and Titian Peale), and the picture now hangs in London's National Portrait Gallery. The *en brosse* hairstyle apart, Waterton's face is a noble one, slightly pained in expression but giving no hint of the reputation that clung to it. As an outstanding naturalist it was reasonable to include in the picture the small crested finch which cheekily balances on his forefinger. And as one with advanced theories about taxidermy why not an example of his work? But only Waterton, with his unerring tendency to the absurd, would have chosen to share his canvas with the decapitated head of an ever so doleful tabby cat.

Born in 1782 the heir to Walton Hall, he could – and frequently did – claim that his family was one of the most ancient in England. Watertons had fought at Crécy and Agincourt, been mentioned in Shakespeare's *Richard II*, taken the field at Marston Moor, and defended Walton Hall itself against Oliver Cromwell. Rather further back, family tradition numbered some seven crowned heads, and as many canonised saints, amongst the Waterton progenitors. (They ranged from the Empress Anna of Russia in the ninth century to St Louis of France in the thirteenth.) Relics of another saint and antecedent, St Thomas More, were kept in the private chapel of Walton Hall. 'Up to the reign of Henry VIII, things had gone on swimmingly for the Watertons'; but the family did not take kindly to innovations, religious or political. The Reformation of 'Harry the eighth, our royal goat', the Commonwealth of Oliver Cromwell, and the dispossession of James II by 'that sordid foreigner' William of Orange were all dismissed by the inmates of Walton Hall as shocking examples of national degeneracy. Staunchly Catholic, Royalist and Jacobite, they saw themelves as the guardians of good old English tradition. And though barred from office, heavily fined, and occasionally imprisoned, they remained proud and respected members of Yorkshire's conservative gentry.

Young Charles was no exception. As he later declared, 'I myself would rather run the risk of going to hell with St Edward the Confessor, the Venerable Bede and St Thomas of Canterbury, than make a dash at heaven in the company of Henry VIII, Queen Bess and Dutch William.' He was sent to a local school – where he learnt nothing, though 'attaining a vast proficiency in the art of finding birds' nests' – and then to the recently opened Jesuit school at Stonyhurst. There he continued to devote himself to zoological studies; but the good fathers perceived that this was something more than just a schoolboy's reaction to the boredom of the classroom. Waterton's passion for the feathered and four-footed might amount to science; it certainly had its uses, and was soon accommodated to the satisfaction of all parties.

The school contained 'an abundance of prog' and was consequently overrun with rats.

'The abilities which I showed in curtailing the careers of these voracious intruders did not fail to bring me into considerable notice.... By a mutual understanding I was considered rat-catcher to the establishment, and also fox-taker, fourmart-killer, and crossbow-charger at the time when the young rooks were fledged. Moreover I filled the duties of organ-blower and football maker with entire satisfaction to the public.

I was now at the height of my ambition.

> Poteras jam, Cadme, videri
> . . . felix.

I followed up my calling with great success. The vermin disappeared by the dozen, the books were moderately well-thumbed and, according to my notion of things, all went on perfectly right.'

The indulgent attitude of the Jesuits was amply repaid. Waterton never once questioned his faith and, to judge by his frequent use of Latin quotations, did more than just thumb the books. He emerged the loyalest of old boys with scarcely a year passing in which he did not visit the Alma Mater or record in print his debt to the Society of Jesus.

In the wisdom of time he would cultivate a very different attitude to the rook, the fox and the fourmart. But against the rat or, to be more precise, *Rattus norvegicus*, he waged a lifelong vendetta of unsurpassed ferocity. Spreading death with poison, traps and predators, he was like the bubonic plague in reverse – except that, to a Waterton, this most wretched of creatures was not simply the Norwegian, or Brown, rat but 'the Hanoverian rat'. His father had it on good evidence that the first of the species to blight British soil had disembarked from the very same ship which brought George I from Hanover. The lesson was plain; and while the Watertons reluctantly concurred in the establishment of the new dynasty, they vented their Jacobite resentment with a savage glee on the Hanoverians' long-tailed minions. It was a rearguard action like most of those in which the Watertons engaged. By the late eighteenth century *Rattus norvegicus* had multiplied prodigiously and all but exterminated the smaller indigenous species. When, at long last, Waterton did come face to face with a solitary specimen of *Rattus rattus* he could scarcely check a tear. 'Poor injured Briton! Hard indeed has been the fate of thy family! In another generation at farthest it will probably sink down to the dust forever.'

Leaving school, he spent a year at home and in 1802 was packed off to Spain to visit two expatriate uncles. On the high seas he was instrumental in fending off a mutiny, he got lost in Cadiz, and he studied the apes on the rock of Gibraltar. The uncles were settled at Malaga and there a pleasant year was whiled away in bird-watching and learning Spanish. He was about to leave when 'the black vomit' – evidently yellow fever – made its appearance. 'Every succeeding day brought testimony that things were not as they ought to be', reported the young Waterton with masterly under-statement. Bodies were piling up in the streets, death-carts rattled over the cobbles, and one's guest at lunch might be dead in his bed by the morning. The city was sealed off and Charles himself was seized with vomiting, fever and 'the most dreadful spasms'. He pulled through; but fourteen thousand did not – including one of his uncles who was buried in a communal grave ('a Spanish marquess lay just below him'). The epidemic was followed by an earthquake which sent the survivors scurrying naked onto the streets; Waterton just had time to pull on his 'unmentionables'. Outside, the scene of misery at last got home to him. 'I now began to think it high time to fly.'

Safely back within the moat of Walton Hall, any lesser mortal might have been tempted to raise the drawbridge, scene of that skirmish with Oliver Cromwell, and abjure travel forever. But Waterton was not yet ready for rural domesticity. He was, moreover, still weak from the after-effects of the fever. So many travellers and explorers first visited the scene of their future labours with the idea of convalescing that it almost amounts to a convention. But Waterton's case was genuine enough. On the voyage back from Spain he had caught a cold which 'attacked the lungs' and almost killed him. Yorkshire's icy winds threatened a recurrence. He needed the sun and, before another winter closed in, he was heading for it. His destination was Demerara.

Some years before, his aunt, a lady of great beauty, had been spotted in the streets of Wakefield by a Mr Daly from Guiana. Such improbable meetings were not at all improbable when Watertons were concerned and invariably proved of consequence. In due course Mr Daly sought and won the hand of Miss Waterton and thus began the family association with the planting fraternity of what is now Guyana. When Charles, aged twenty-three, headed for South America it was to manage the family plantations, now three in number, near Georgetown. What Georgetown – or Starbroek, as its recent Dutch owners had known it – was like in 1805 it is hard to imagine. Waterton gives few clues. Right from the start he was only interested in the wildlife.

'Whilst I was on the estates I had the finest opportunity in the world of examining the waterfowl of Guiana; they were in vast abundance all along the sea-shore, and in the fresh-water swamps behind the plantations. No country in the world can offer a more extensive and fertile field to the ornithologist than our celebrated colony of Demerara.'

With some pride he records serving in the colony's militia and undertaking a couple of confused and not very productive missions of a semi-official character. Otherwise he concentrated on the birds. Many of the observations in his subsequent journeys must be attributed to this period and, likewise, the anecdotes; even a Waterton could hardly have crammed so many bizarre encounters with the animal kingdom into the short forays which followed his eight years on the plantations.

A foretaste of what was to come was provided by an archetypal encounter with a labari snake which occurred during a mission to the Spanish Governor of the neighbouring Orinoco. Tacking upriver in a schooner provided by the Spaniards Waterton spied a deadly labari, or jacarara, coiled up in a bush on the bank. He fired, wounding but not killing it. Then 'being wishful to dissect it,' he lunged into the bush with the idea of grabbing the serpent by the throat and stowing it aboard. The helmsman objected and put the boat about. Waterton was left clinging to a branch which dipped him in and out of the water, a tempting bait to passing alligators; the snake looked blearily on. A more pitiful situation it is hard to imagine and it was this extraordinary ingenuity of misadventure which would distinguish all his exploits in pursuit of science. Eventually the crew took pity on him. The boat drew alongside and the dripping traveller clambered aboard. But not before securing his trophy. 'It measured eight feet in length. As soon as I had got a change of clothes, I killed it and made a dissection of the head.'

Such exploits, when presented to the 'closet naturalists' at home, were liable to be misunderstood. Waterton would be accused of 'a constant propensity to dress truth in the garb of fiction'. His response was to invite his critics to consider each incident carefully; if anyone still suspected him of deviating from the truth they were to present themselves in person and he was sure that he would soon convince them otherwise. Needless to say, the challenge was not accepted; but neither did it stem the tide of disbelief.

As for the traveller's agility, not to say foolhardiness, in invariably coming into physical contact with his specimens, he had this to say:

'Some of my encounters with wild beasts may appear hair-breadth escapes, and very alarming things, to readers at their own fire-sides; but to me in the forest they appeared not so . . . I was well fitted out for adventure. I went expressly to look for wild beasts and, having found them, it would have been impossible for me to have refrained from coming into actual contact with them.'

Other naturalists might have contented themselves with careful observation of the animals, but Waterton had to come to grips with them – literally. Charles Darwin, another youthful rat-catcher and a future admirer of Waterton, was still in his infancy – and so was natural history. The object of the exercise was not study but specimen collection. And if the specimen could be procured without being actually blown to bits, so much the better for taxidermy and science. Waterton had neither the equipment nor the time for trapping; if a bait was needed he preferred to offer himself.

In 1812 he finally gave up the management of the family plan-tations to concentrate on his scientific interests. His father was now dead, and he had succeeded to the title by which he would become best known, the Squire of Walton. The Walton Hall estate was not vast but it assured him of a moderate income for the rest of his life. He was free to indulge his whims. The first of these was to penetrate the interior of Guiana as far as the frontier with Portuguese territory, now Brazil.

Ostensibly the object of this journey was to procure samples of a deadly poison which he called 'wourali' and which we know as curare. He was also keen to share his enthusiasm for the South American jungle and to promote its claims as a paradise for naturalists. With this in view he hit on the novel idea of writing his narrative in the second person singular. Asides addressed to 'the courteous reader' were not unusual in the literature of the day; but few writers can have taken this convention to such tortuous lengths:

'If, in the cool of the evening, thou hast been tempted to stray too far from thy place of abode, and art deprived of light to write down the information which thou hast collected, the fire-fly, which thou wilt see in almost every bush around thee, will be thy candle. Hold it over thy pocket book in any position which thou knowest will not hurt it, and it will afford thee ample light. And when thou hast done with it, put it kindly back again on the next branch to thee. It will want no other reward for its services.'

Aware, perhaps, that this arch approach was somehow prejudicing his otherwise vivid descriptions of jungle life, he tried the second person plural. Still the result was unsatisfactory.

'The Indian place you are now at is not the proper place to have come to in order to reach the Portuguese frontiers. You have advanced too much to the westward. But there was no alternative. The ground betwixt you and another small settlement (which was the right place to have gone to) was overflowed; and thus, instead of proceeding southward, you were obliged to wind along the foot of the western hills, quite out of your way.'

This, as the author himself was wont to remark, 'would not do'. At last he settled for the first person. But by then he had already conducted the 'courteous reader' some four hundred miles up the Demerara and Essequibo rivers, and was approaching his destination, the Portuguese fort of San Joaquim on the Rio Branco tributary of the Amazon. For a solitary white man the journey was a considerable feat and represents the Squire's only claim to fame as an explorer. Unfortunately, to conform with the 'courteous reader' style, such geographical information as he lets slip reads more like a series of clues in a treasure hunt. He added nothing to the maps of the day and even with a modern map his route defies elucidation.

Of considerably greater interest were his descriptions of the flora and fauna. The trees, animals and, above all, the birds, he listed and described with avid delight. Much of what he had to say was new to science and, to the general reader, his evocation of the colours and sounds of the tropical jungle must have come as a revelation – even when marred by an excess of Waterton whimsy:

'When in thy hammock, should the thought of thy little crosses and disappointments, in thy ups and downs through life, break in upon thee, and throw thee into a pensive mood, the owl will bear thee company. She will tell thee that hard has been her fate too; and at intervals "whip-poor-Will" and "Willy-come go" [nightjars] will take up the tale of sorrow.'

Most of the forest was uninhabited but in the more open country near the Portuguese frontier Waterton rejoiced to make the acquaintance of the Macoushi Indians. These were the people whose curare poison was reputedly the most lethal. It was said that a Macoushi arrow or dart (from a blow-pipe) killed man or beast instantaneously. Was ever poison so deadly? And, if so, what were its ingredients? Waterton was soon happily buying and testing the fatal dose as if it were some panacea. Indeed, he thought curare might be of some medicinal significance. The interesting thing about it was that the victim appeared to expire without spasms or pain. Might it not then be the relaxing antidote for a convulsive disease like rabies? His friend, Mr Sewell of the London Veterinary College, was certainly of this opinion.

The prospect of perhaps benefiting mankind helped inure the Squire to the very uncongenial business of animal experiments. Hens, dogs, a three-toed sloth and even an ox were sacrificed. The poison worked splendidly; the hens lasted barely five minutes, the sloth slumped into oblivion at the eleventh minute, and the ox, well-fed and 'from nine hundred to a thousand pounds in weight', died with a few unscheduled convulsions at the twenty-fifth. 'His flesh was very sweet and savoury at dinner.' (The poison had no effect on the meat.)

Considering that the Macoushi recipe included not only the curare vine, *Strychnos toxifera*, but also two species of stinging ant, the fangs of a couple of poisonous snakes, some toxic vegetable matter and 'a quantity of the strongest Indian pepper', these dramatic results were not unexpected. But sadly the Macoushi antidotes – immersion in water and heavy doses of honey – proved less than effective. Waterton determined to continue his experiments in more congenial and scientific surroundings. Carefully sealing his treasure in wax balls, he headed for home.

Malaria, or rather 'a tertian ague', had already overtaken him in San Joaquim. Now, on the return journey, he again became seriously ill 'so that to all appearance his last day's march was over' (the Squire was now experimenting with the third person singular). He just made it to a friend's plantation near the mouth of the Demerara, rested there briefly, and then sailed for England and a long convalescence.

'For three revolving autumns, the ague-beaten wanderer never saw, without a sigh, the swallow bend her flight towards warmer regions. He wished to go too, but could not; for sickness had enfeebled him and prudence pointed out the folly of roving again, too soon, across the northern tropic.'

He consoled himself by undertaking some well publicised experiments with the curare. The victims now were donkeys and the venue the Veterinary College in London. The first donkey was inoculated in the leg and died in twelve minutes. A second, similarly inoculated but with a tourniquet just above the wound, went about its business with unconcern until the bandage was removed. It then died in ten minutes. Number three was injected in the shoulder and again appeared to breathe its last in the tenth minute. But this time the Squire was well prepared.

'An incision was then made in its windpipe and through it the lungs were regularly inflated for two hours with a pair of bellows. Suspended animation returned. The ass held up her head and looked around; but the inflating being discontinued, she sunk once more in apparent death. The artificial breathing was again recommenced, and continued without intermission for two hours more. This saved the ass from final dissolution; she rose up and walked about; she seemed neither in agitation nor in pain.'

For a year the donkey, like the Squire, continued far from well. But the kindly Duke of Northumberland, one of Waterton's most influential patrons, arranged for her to be sent down to Walton Hall and there, 'by midsummer, she became fat and frisky'. The Squire called her Wouralia. 'Wouralia shall be sheltered from the wintry storm; and when summer comes she shall feed in the finest pasture. No burden shall be placed upon her, and she shall end her days in peace.' She did just that in 1839, twenty-five years after the curare experiment.

Given the success of inflation as a restorative, the next move was to try the poison on a rabies victim. In 1830 a constable in Nottingham, by name Phelps, rescued a small dog stuck down a man-hole and got bitten for his pains. Constable Phelps was a man after Waterton's heart, an animal lover, a respected guardian of the law, and a courageous individual. Feeling unwell and recognising the cause, Phelps said goodbye to his wife and children and to his colleagues at the station, admitted himself to the local surgery, and invited the Nottingham medical fraternity to do with him what they could. Various were the remedies tried without success before someone recalled the Squire of Walton and his curare. An express was sent off to Wakefield and the Squire hastened to the scene. But, alas, too late. Poor Phelps was dead when he arrived.

Another series of reasonably successful donkey experiments ensued. No further mention, though, is made of human experiments and this may be significant. Ingenious as the curare cure was, it was never to win medical acceptance.

While 'the ague-beaten wanderer' had been conducting his

first donkey experiments, unexpected recognition of his standing as a traveller and naturalist had come from Lord Bathurst, the Colonial Secretary. Waterton, like Mungo Park, Thomas Manning and almost every other early nineteenth-century traveller, had been encouraged by Sir Joseph Banks, President of the Royal Society. No doubt Banks had a hand in canvassing his eligibility as an official traveller, and Waterton was indeed gratified by the Colonial Secretary's interest. But he patently lacked that ruthless ambition which distinguished the professional explorer. When Lord Bathurst offered him the chance of investigating the natural productions of Madagascar and the Seychelles he accepted, then resigned the commission lamely pleading ill-health. This was not behaviour calculated to endear him to the authorities and, apart from vetoing another Banks initiative – to the Congo in 1817 – he never again found official favour.

Instead he went his own way and in 1816, discharging himself as at last fit for action, sailed again for South America. His destination this time was Pernambuco – now Recife – on the horn of Brazil. The Squire could find little to recommend the place. The streets were filthy and the town-planning non-existent. His beloved Jesuits had suffered even at the hands of the Portuguese and their college was now being used to stable an elephant. In the botanical gardens, while pursuing a flock of white-spotted orioles, he came face to face with a rattlesnake; 'an instantaneous spring backwards prevented fatal consequences'. And when the rains set in and the birds started to moult, he decided he had had enough.

'It was time to proceed elsewhere. The conveyance to the interior was by horses; and this mode, together with the heavy rains, would expose preserved specimens to almost certain damage. The journey to Maranhao by land would take at least forty days. The route was not wild enough to engage the attention of an explorer, or civilised enough to afford common comforts to a traveller. By sea there were no opportunities except slave ships. As the transporting of poor Negroes from port to port for sale pays well in Brazil, the ships' decks were crowded with them. This would not do.'

Overcoming this objection, he boarded a brig for Cayenne in French Guiana. The vessel had 'poor accommodations' and Waterton made his bed on top of a hen-coop on deck. 'Even here an unsavoury little beast, called bug, was neither shy nor deficient in appetite.'

After fourteen days Cayenne hove into sight. The plan now was to transfer to a sloop and back-track to the Amazon for what would surely have been 'a journey wild enough for an explorer'. He would sail up the Amazon and the Rio Negro, strike out north for the Essequibo and thus back to Georgetown. Unfortunately, though, the coastal currents were not in his favour. The Amazon was in spate and it would take weeks just to enter it. Moreover, he could not afford to wait in French Guiana for 'this was not the time for a traveller to enjoy Cayenne'. As a result of Napoleon's defeat at Waterloo the colony had been taken over by the Portuguese and was still in some confusion. The Squire therefore changed his plans once again and hastened on to neighbouring Surinam (Dutch Guiana). There he made a brief foray into the interior before finally repairing to Demerara and Georgetown.

Lest the reader of his travelogue should suppose that this second journey had been an unmitigated failure, Waterton now abandoned any pretence at narrative in favour of another long eulogy on Demerara and further descriptions of its fauna. He claims to have spent six months ornithologising before finally sailing for England, although the absence of incident, as much as the confused chronology, leave this in doubt.

As usual his observations on the birds are a delight. The flight of the toucan, he reports, 'is by jerks'. Toucans and toucanets are 'social but not gregarious' and 'you will be at a loss to conjecture for what ends nature has overloaded the head of this bird with such an enormous bill'. The Squire himself could offer no explanation, but one day, while tucking into a dinner of boiled toucan, he did conceive a new way of preserving the vivid colours of the bill. No doubt a toucan, with its great beak as bright as life, was amongst the two hundred stuffed specimens he took home.

This discovery was followed by a spirited defence of the woodpecker. 'Why do you hunt me up and down for an imaginary offence?' declared the poor bird at the Squire's prompting. 'I have never spoiled a leaf of your property, much less your wood.' Far from damaging sound timber the woodpecker actually rendered the woodsman a service by pin-pointing – or puncturing – those trees which were unsound. Likewise the goatsucker, 'that poor, injured little bird of the night'. It had never stolen a drop of goat's milk in its life; it simply preyed on the flies that molested the herds.

From the vulture to the wren, Waterton catalogued the merits of what he invariably called 'the feathered tribe'. Some birds performed a service, others delighted the eye or the ear, others were good to eat. He would kill for the pot and he would kill for specimens but never for sport. A wide-eyed joy permeates his descriptions of plumage, song and behaviour. Conservation was scarcely a live issue in Guiana, but Waterton's simple delight in observing and characterising each of the forests' myriad of species, and asserting its right to an independent existence, was a novelty in itself.

He was still, and would forever remain, the tree-climbing schoolboy whose passion for the outdoors was prompted more by a wayward and inquisitive nature than by scientific dedication. He rambled through the forests barefoot and recommended any other South American traveller to do the same.

'Leave behind you your high-seasoned dishes, your wines and your delicacies; carry nothing but what is necessary for your own comfort and the object in view, and depend upon your own skill or that of an Indian for fish and game. A sheet, about twelve feet long, ten wide, painted, and with loop holes on each side, will be of great service; in a few minutes you can suspend it betwixt two trees in the shape of a roof. Under this, in your hammock, you may defy the pelting shower, and sleep heedless of the dews of night. A hat, a shirt, and a light pair of trousers, will be all the raiment you require. Custom will soon teach you to tread lightly and barefoot on the little inequalities of the ground and show you how to pass on, unwounded, amid the mantling briars. . . . The youth who incautiously reels into the lobby of Drury Lane, after leaving the table sacred to the god of wine, is exposed to more certain ruin, sickness and decay than he who wanders a whole year in the wilds of Demerara.'

As with the fauna, so with the natives. The important thing was to respect their customs and to be eternally affable, considerate and appreciative. 'To feel, as it were, at home amongst them is the sure way to enable you to pass merrily on.' Such unusual sentiments so impressed Sir Joseph Banks that he commended them as 'far excelling, in real utility, everything I have hitherto seen'. But few indeed were the travellers who would emulate them.

With nothing worse this time than a mild 'quartan ague', the Squire returned home in the summer of 1817. In the ensuing winter he made a pilgrimage to Rome of which little is recorded. Yet this journey occasioned one of the most notorious of Waterton adventures and, laconic as his narrative is, only the Squire's own words can commend its authenticity.

'During our stay in the Eternal City I fell in with my old friend and school-fellow, Captain Jones. Many a tree had we climbed together in the last century; and, as our nerves were in excellent trim, we mounted to the top of St Peter's, ascended the cross, and then climbed thirteen feet higher, where we reached the point of the conductor, and left our gloves upon it. After this we visited the castle of St Angelo and contrived to get on the head of the guardian angel, where we stood on one leg.'

Pope Pius VII was not amused. The story goes that he personally ordered the removal of the gloves. When no Roman steeplejack would volunteer for the task, Waterton himself obligingly returned to the scene and duly made a second ascent. But perhaps the more endearing and memorable extravagance is that image of the Captain and the Squire posing one-legged, like storks, on the head of the gigantic gilded angel on the Castel Sant'Angelo. Would that the camera had been invented a few decades earlier.

On the journey back from Rome the Squire got his come-uppance. 'As bad luck would have it', he contrived to put his knee through the plate-glass window of his carriage while clambering aloft to inspect the luggage. This happened in the middle of the night on Mont Cenis. With the aid of a lamp he plucked out splinters of glass; some, though, must have remained within the wound. A fever set in. By the time he reached Paris the leg was 'in a deplorable condition', and though medical treatment there and in London saved it from amputation, it remained stiff for nearly two years. The long convalescence kept him at Walton Hall. A number of surprising innovations in the running of the estate probably date from this period. But all the while 'Guiana', as he chose to put it, 'still whispered in my ear and seemed to invite me once more to wander through her distant forests.' In February 1820 he could contain himself no longer. He sailed from the Clyde on his third, and far and away his most eventful, journey to South America.

The narrative of this journey, a mere fifty pages long, is Waterton's masterpiece. At last he abandons all pretence at writing a guidebook/prospectus and, with profuse apologies, introduces 'that unwelcome monosyllable, I'. The change of style pays immediate dividends. Suddenly all the restraints self-imposed on a born raconteur are removed. With a grand disregard for everything except the rattling good tale, he presents one of the most bizarre, incredible, and inconsequential collections of incidents and observations ever recorded.

In 1820 it was Georgetown's turn for the Black Vomit, now called yellow fever. The Squire hastened through, and ascended the Demerara river to Mibiri creek. There, in the derelict mansion of an old friend, he slung his hammock and set up base. From the deserted rooms numerous frogs and snakes were expelled 'without buffet or rebuke' ('their world was before them'). The owls betook themselves to a hollow tree and only 'the bats and vampires staid with me and went in and out as usual'. The behaviour of the bats soon became his major field for study, for he had scarcely set up home before he was confined to hammock by a vicious ague.

'A cruel headache, thirst and a pain in the small of the back, informed me what the case was. . . . that I was going to have a tight brush of it, and that I ought to meet it with becoming fortitude. I dozed, and woke, and started, and then dozed again, and suddenly awoke thinking I was falling down a precipice. . . . I took ten grains of calomel and a scruple of jalap and drank during the day large quantities of tea, weak and warm. At five in the evening the pulse had risen to a hundred and thirty, and the headache was almost insupportable, especially on looking to right or left. I now opened a vein and made a large orifice to allow the blood to rush out rapidly. I closed it after losing sixteen ounces.'

Blood-letting – or 'tapping the claret' – was the Squire's answer to most maladies and in later life became something of an addiction. He was said never to feel the pain of the lancet and to be able to perform the operation on either arm single-handed. Now, as later, it afforded instant relief. The fever and headache abated and with the help of a large dose of home-made castor oil and regular ministrations of quinine he recovered.

But not for long. Whilst in hot pursuit of a red-headed woodpecker he trod, barefoot, on a sharp stump and was carried back to his hammock for another three weeks. The damaged foot needed a poultice; 'as heat and moisture are the two principal virtues of a poultice, nothing could produce these two qualities better than fresh cow-dung boiled'. With the foot thus bandaged, but with the toes sticking invitingly out, Waterton lay back to study the vampires.

'As there was a free entrance and exit to the vampire in the loft where I slept I had many a fine opportunity of paying attention to this nocturnal surgeon. The vampire in general measures about twenty-six inches from wing to wing extended, though I once killed one which measured thirty-two inches. He does not always live on blood. When the moon shone bright and the fruit of the banana tree was ripe, I could see him approach and eat it.'

This was most disappointing. To have one's toes shunned by a vampire in favour of bananas, and this at a time when more blood-letting would surely have benefited him – was this not the cruellest of ironies? Correctly he observed that 'the vampires' seemed to be of two different species. But he never realised that the larger, the one that inhabited his loft, was not a vampire at all but an exclusively vegetarian species of bat.

What with one thing and another the first weeks at Mibiri Creek were best forgotten. But one important discovery did result. Whilst tossing in his hammock he considered the inadequacies of taxidermy as then practised and came up with a novel solution. The problem was that stuffed specimens invariably shrank. Where the animal had a good pelt the resultant wrinkling did not show, but on more hairless areas, like the face, this shrinkage resulted in hideous deformities. Waterton's solution involved soaking the skins in 'corrosive sublimate' and virtually remodelling them. It was complex and time-consuming. But it was also highly successful. And to prove the point what better subject than that baldest of creatures, the snake.

As the Squire sat reading a pocket edition of Horace on the steps of his crumbling mansion, word at last arrived that a large snake had been found. Examination showed it to be a boa constrictor, fourteen feet long and immensely thick. It was not poisonous but thanks to the 'wonderful extension' of its jaws, it could as easily swallow an attacker as crush him.

'Aware that the day was on the decline, and that the approach of night would be detrimental to the dissection, a thought struck me that I could take him alive. I imagined that if I could strike him with my lance behind his head and pin him to the ground, I might succeed in capturing him.'

The two Negroes who had accompanied him were not enthusiastic about this plan. They offered to go for his gun. To secure their co-operation, as much as to ensure that the skin was not damaged, Waterton saw fit to disarm them. 'If I might judge from their physiognomies, they seemed to consider this as a most intolerable act of tyranny in me.'

Lance at the ready, the Squire then inched forward. The snake did not move. He drove the lance at its neck and pinned it to the ground.

'That moment the Negro next to me seized the lance and held it firm in its place, while I dashed head foremost into the den to grapple with the snake, and to get hold of his tail before he could do any mischief. On pinning him to the ground with the lance he gave a tremendous hiss. . . . We had a sharp fray in the den, the rotten sticks flying on all sides, and each party struggling for superiority. I called out to the second Negro to throw himself upon me, as I found I was not heavy enough. He did so, and the additional weight was of great service. I had now got firm hold of his tail; and after a violent struggle or two he gave in, finding himself overpowered. This was the moment to secure him. I contrived to unloose my braces and with them tied up the snake's mouth.'

The snake, 'finding himself in an unpleasant situation', redoubled his efforts and continued to writhe as the three men bore him triumphantly back to base. By now the light was too far gone for dissection. The snake was therefore deposited in an enormous sack and dumped beneath the Squire's hammock. 'I cannot say he allowed me to have a quiet night. He was very restless and fretful; and had Medusa been my wife, there could not have been more continued and disagreeable hissing in the bed-chamber that night.'

Next morning, with ten assistants, he untied the sack and reclaimed his braces. 'Nothing serious occurred.' The snake bled like an ox when its throat was cut and dissection took all day. The skin was still being treated when, a week later, while following a new species of parakeet, the Squire fell in with yet another boa. This one was smaller, about ten feet long. Waterton was alone and unarmed, but 'there was not a moment to lose'. He dropped to the ground and grabbed it by the tail.

'The snake instantly turned, and came on at me, with his head about a yard from the ground as if to ask me what business I had to take liberties with his tail. I let him come, hissing and open-mouthed, within two feet of my face, and then, with all the force I was master of, I drove my fist, shielded by my hat, full in his jaws. He was stunned and confounded by the blow, and ere he could recover himself, I had seized him by the throat with both hands, in such a position that he could not bite me; I then allowed him to coil himself round my body, and marched off with him as my lawful prize. He pressed me hard but not alarmingly so.'

The Squire was now ready to tackle anything. His great ambition had long been to catch a live cayman; and for the man who had wrestled with one boa constrictor and knocked out another, such a feat appeared by no means impossible. But the cayman was not to be found round Mibiri Creek. He therefore turned his attention to more scientific matters. As might be guessed, he had a particular interest in nature's freaks. The stealthy jaguar and the cheeky monkey attracted him not half as much as the bumbling armadillo and the independent and inoffensive ant-eater. This latter he studied minutely. He was the first to observe that, without a tooth in its mouth, it neither chewed nor sucked but relied on an adhesive secretion which coated its long and inquisitive tongue. At the risk of much ridicule he also claimed that drawings of the ant-eater which showed it walking on the soles of its feet were incorrect. The ant-eater walked on the outside edge of its feet with its claws folded into a fist 'with somewhat the appearance of a club-hand'.

Still more contentious, but equally correct, were the improbable claims that he made for another obvious Waterton favourite – the sloth.

'Those who have written on this singular animal have remarked that he is in a perpetual state of pain, that he is proverbially slow in his movements, that he is a prisoner in space, and that as soon as he has consumed all the leaves of the tree upon which he had mounted, he rolls himself up in the form of a ball and then falls to the ground. This is not the case.'

Like other quadrupeds, the sloth was commonly represented as standing on its four legs. Even the stuffed specimen in the British Museum was standing thus. But this, too, was 'not the case'. After observing these shy creatures in the forests, and after actually keeping one in his room for several months, Waterton pronounced what to many must have seemed a sheer absurdity – that the sloth belonged not on the ground but in the trees and that he stood not on his feet but hung upside down. 'He moves suspended from the branch, he rests suspended from it, and he sleeps suspended from it.' This discovery immediately accounted for what otherwise seemed his 'bungled conformation' and entitled 'the poor fellow' to a reappraisal. In his native element, dense forest, he was far from slothful and moved 'with wonderful rapidity'. 'I stood looking on, lost in amazement at his singular mode of progress.' Waterton was the first man to give a correct idea of the sloth's life-style, though not until several years later when the London Zoo acquired a live one was he widely believed.

A sloth was amongst his tally of stuffed specimens from this third journey. So too were two hundred and thirty birds, five armadillos, two tortoises, the two boa constrictors, a solitary ant-eater, and, at long last and very far from least, a fully grown cayman. Despairing of ever finding a large alligator in Mibiri Creek, the Squire had staked all on a short expedition up the Essequibo. In Georgetown he bought heavy-duty fishing gear – chain, ropes and shark hooks – then sailed upriver. Four days later the party made camp and commenced fishing. The caymans – 'caymen' as Waterton preferred – were there all right, sliding through the water like large black logs and emitting 'a singular and awful sound . . . like a suppressed sigh, so loud that you might hear it above a mile off'. They relished the large fish used as bait, but they showed no inclination to swallow the shark hooks. On four consecutive nights the bait was simply removed.

'I was now convinced that something was materially wrong.' In search of new ideas, he repaired to the nearest Indian village. There, over a dinner of boiled ant-eater and red monkey ('the monkey was very good indeed but the ant-eater had been kept beyond its time') the Indians obligingly offered to act as ghillies. They produced their own version of a cayman hook, changed the bait from fish to rabbit, and were immediately successful.

'About half-past five in the morning an Indian stole off silently to take a look at the bait. On arriving at the place he set up a tremendous shout. We all jumped from our hammocks and ran to him. The Indians got there before me, for they had no clothes to put on and I lost two minutes in looking for my trousers and slipping into them.'

The line was tight, the hook firm and the monster had gone below. But the problem was, as always in those pre-anaesthetic days, how to overcome him without damaging his skin. The Indians wanted to immobilise him with arrows, and his own Negroes were all for going for the gun. But Waterton was adamant. He had not come three hundred miles for a mutilated skin. 'They wanted to kill him and I wanted to take him alive.'

A possible solution was suggested by the eight-foot mast of his canoe:

'It appeared clear to me that if I went down upon one knee, and held the mast in the same position as the soldier holds his bayonet when rushing to the charge, I could force it down the cayman's throat when he came open mouthed at me. When this was told to the Indians they brightened up, and said they would help me to pull him out of the river. "Brave squad", said I to myself, "Audax omnia perpeti now that you have got me betwixt yourselves and danger". I then mustered all hands for the last time before the battle. We were four South American savages, two Negroes from Africa, a creole from Trinidad, and myself, a white man from Yorkshire.'

The Squire took up position, the natives hauled on the rope, and the cayman broke the surface. It was ten and a half feet long.

'I saw enough not to fall in love at first sight. I now told them we would run all risks and have him on land immediately. They pulled again and out he came – "monstrum, horrende, informe". This was an interesting moment. I kept my position firmly with my eye fixed steadfastly upon him.

'By the time the cayman was within two yards of me I saw that he was in a state of fear and perturbation; I instantly dropped the mast, sprang up, and jumped on his back, turning half round as I vaulted so that I gained my seat with my face in a right position. I immediately seized his forelegs, twisted them on his back; thus they served me for a bridle.

'He now seemed to have recovered from his surprise and prob-ably fancying himself in hostile company, he began to plunge furiously and lashed the sand behind with his long and powerful tail. I was out of reach of it by being near his head. He continued to plunge and strike, and made my seat very uncomfortable. I must have been a fine sight for an unoccupied spectator.'

The Squire was reminded of Arion's ride on the dolphin. And though he later claimed that it involved no more than 'any old lady, minus her crinoline, might have done', he also acknowledged the experience gained in youth when riding to Lord Darlington's foxhounds. The cayman continued to plunge and thrash but, using something stronger than the jockey's braces, the jaw was eventually tied up and the front legs lashed together. Thus bound, the reptile was conveyed back to camp by boat. 'There I cut his throat; and after breakfast was over, dissection commenced.'

A more fitting conclusion to his most productive journey could not have been hoped for. The Squire had not only captured a live cayman, but ridden it. It was the climax of his close encounters with the animal kingdom, and on this winning note he returned to Georgetown and, in April 1821, took ship to Liverpool. He was now forty-one. Age neither dulled his spirits nor quelled his energy; this was by no means the end of his travels. But it was his last pioneering effort.

Back in England his euphoria was soon eclipsed. The boxes

containing all his specimens were impounded by customs officials pending payment of duty on an absurdly high valuation. The Squire remonstrated and ranted to no avail. Eventually he paid up; but, by way of revenge, decided not to divulge his long-awaited discoveries in taxidermy nor to make his skill available to others. Instead he immersed himself in the affairs of Walton Hall estate.

To many, Charles Waterton's reputation as traveller, taxidermist, naturalist and eccentric is second to his standing as a conservationist. It has been claimed that he was the first Englishman to concern himself with the preservation of native fauna for any purpose other than sport, and that Walton Hall was the first-ever conservation park. To both claims there is much substance.

Within the precincts of the estate firearms were banned and no creature – with, of course, the exception of the Hanoverian rat – was considered fair game. To make his point the Squire now commenced fortifying the place with an eight-foot wall. This was no mean undertaking. The wall had to be three miles long and cost some £10,000. It took four years to build, in part due to his piggy bank approach to finance. He had a horror of debt and a deep distrust of paper money. The project therefore had to be financed out of income and paid for in gold. As soon as £500 in sovereigns had accumulated in his drawer the masons were summoned and the wall advanced. When the sovereigns were exhausted work stopped and the men were laid off until the drawer could be replenished.

Neither the wall, nor what went on behind it, met with universal approval. To the Squire it was cause for congratulation that 'I turn loose upon the public three score carrion crows a year'. His farming neighbours disagreed. To them as to most contemporaries, British birds were of just two sorts – game and vermin. Both resorted to the sanctuary of Walton Hall in large numbers, hotly pursued by keepers and poachers. Against the latter Waterton waged a sustained war comparable with that against the Hanoverian rat. But nightly patrols and the occasional fisticuffs failed to discourage them. In desperation he hit on the novel idea of filling his woods with life-like decoys, 'Six or seven dozen of wooden pheasants, nailed to the branches of trees in the surrounding woods cause unutterable vexation and loss of ammunition to these amateurs of nocturnal plunder.'

On the more positive side, the trees were also filled with nesting boxes and he contrived a variety of other nesting sites for everything from the starling to the swan. Observations played a large part in his studies; a powerful telescope in the drawing-room gave him endless hours of delight and his regular rounds included climbing the loftiest of trees. The tendency to go a little further and actually to participate and interfere in nature was less laudable. The Squire had a mischievous habit of swopping eggs from nest to nest so that a magpie might unexpectedly find its fledglings developing into jackdaws. He was obsessed by freaks, a duck with web-less feet being an especial favourite. And on one memorable occasion he conceived the 'crude and undigested idea' that winged flight was not solely the prerogative of bats and birds. He designed and manufactured his own wings, climbed onto one of the farmyard buildings and, still flapping vigorously, crashed headfirst to the ground.

'The knowledge of my rash attempt to confide in wings, together with my failure, which at the time was comparatively in a nutshell, where I hoped it would remain, soon, contrary to my wishes, spread abroad and the rumour, in its route, gathered nothing that was enviable on my behalf, but just the reverse. This was somewhat annoying.'

Perhaps it was as a result of this disappointment that in 1824 he embarked on his fourth journey. His destination was North America although, on the way back, he did revisit Guiana. It was not, however, a field trip and, as Sydney Smith, the most appreciative of his reviewers put it, 'our author does not appear as much at home amongst men as amongst beasts'. He was back within the year, and in 1825 *Wanderings in South America*, the résumé of all four journeys plus, at last, his discoveries in taxidermy, appeared. Its instant success – it was republished four times in his lifetime – was no thanks to the savants and critics, who greeted it with howls of derision. But it said much for the stature of its author as a contemporary freak, as beloved and inoffensive as so many of his animal subjects.

This was not exactly the recognition which the Squire coveted. Nothing enfuriated him more than being dubbed an eccentric. He would call himself 'an independent rover' or 'a private wanderer' but what he really sought was recognition as a naturalist. In disgust he busied himself with the responsibilities of Walton Hall. A matter that required urgent attention (he was now forty-seven) was the provision of an heir. In 1829, therefore, he married Anne Edmonstone; a year later she duly presented him with a son. But this most delicate of transactions was tinged with a tragic poignancy as well as the inevitable absurdity.

Anne Edmonstone was the daughter of his old friend Charles

Edmonstone whose crumbling mansion in Mibiri Creek had been the base for operations during the third journey. Edmonstone had returned to Scotland and there died leaving three daughters. In 1829 they were at school in a convent in Bruges; Anne was just seventeen. Her grandmother had been an Arrowack Indian princess and her father claimed descent from several kings of Scotland as well as from Lady Godiva. To a Waterton, Anne was therefore a most suitable, if young, bride. The proposal was probably made through the Mother Superior of the convent and the wedding took place in the convent chapel at the improbable hour of 4 am. The Squire took his bride back to Walton Hall 'the happiest man in the world'.

'But it pleased heaven to convince me that all felicity here below is no more than a mere illusive transitory dream.' In May 1830 the son and heir was born; three weeks later Anne died. However curious the circumstances of his marriage, his grief at this loss was genuine, copious and private. It is known only that he never again slept in a bed, but always on the floor with a block of wood for a pillow. His lifestyle, always austere, became positively ascetic; he rose at 3.30 am, wore clothes that were little better than rags, and rarely entertained. A picture of St Catherine of Alexandria sat on the mantelpiece of his sitting-room. He thought it resembled Anne and would stare at it for hours, lost in reverie.

Anne's two sisters, Eliza and Helen, themselves little more than children, moved into Walton Hall to keep house and look after the baby. With this strange ménage the Squire was delighted. In outings reminiscent of the tours of Captain and Mrs Thicknesse, he escorted the two girls and young Edmund as far afield as Sicily to study bird migration, and Naples to witness the lique-faction of the blood of Saint Gennaro.

Bereavement neither dampened his ardour as a naturalist nor subdued his love of the preposterous. In addition to the ant-eater, the cayman, the sloth and the boa, Walton Hall was filling up with other no less gruesome creatures. His skill as a taxidermist cried out for something more than mere life-like restoration. As a frontispiece in *Wanderings in South America* he had included a drawing of 'The Nondescript', which was in fact a Red Howler Monkey skilfully remodelled to look like some hideous and hairy hominid. It was intended simply as a demonstration of his skills; but it misfired. Some thought it was a South American man-of-the-woods and in exceptionally bad taste. Those in the know suspected that it was supposed to be a caricature of the Secretary to the Treasury to whom Waterton had had to pay those heavy

Capt. Philip Thicknesse, gentleman, scoundrel and professional tourist

Above: The Thicknesse family on tour. Jocko, the monkey, with pigtail and livery rides postilion, but the parakeet must be hiding in the cabriolet

Right: Thomas Manning, reluctant and reticent traveller

Above: The European factories in Canton, Manning's base for the nine years he spent trying to enter China

Below: Lieut. James Holman shortly after he became blind

Holman in old age. The beard was a relic of his journey round the world

Above: Krasnoi Square (Red Square) in Moscow. Holman measured the walls of the Kremlin by pacing them out

Below: Sledge travel in Russia. Holman and his captor made their mid-winter crossing of Siberia in a similar vehicle

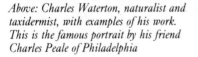

Above: Charles Waterton, naturalist and taxidermist, with examples of his work. This is the famous portrait by his friend Charles Peale of Philadelphia

Right: The 'Nondescript', thought by some to be a caricature of the Secretary to the Treasury and by others to be a self-portrait of Waterton. In fact it was a red howler monkey

The funeral procession of Charles Waterton on the lake at Walton Hall. The first boat contains a bishop and seventeen priests chanting the office of the dead. The deceased's yacht, draped in mourning, takes up the rear

Above: A vampire bat, but not of the same species as that which disdained Waterton's big toe

Below: Waterton astride the cayman. The illustrator has incorrectly included another European and has denied Waterton the braces which served him as a bridle

Above: Waterton saving the day when a rattlesnake escaped during toxaemia experiments at Leeds

Below: Dr Joseph Wolff, curate of High Hoyland and 'Grand Dervish of England, Scotland, Ireland and the whole of Europe and America'

A caricature of Wolff at about the time of his marriage to Lady Georgiana Walpole

*Abdul Samut Khan, the Naib of the Amir of Bukhara and Wolff's most
dangerous adversary during his detention there*

*The elusive William Gifford Palgrave suitably disguised
before entering Arabia*

Above: The oasis of Jauf on Palgrave's route to Riyadh

Below: According to Palgrave, victims of the simoon *or sirocco were suffocated by the heat and the flying sand*

Dr G. W. Leitner, ethnologist, educationalist and explorer – 'genius untempered by judgement'

Above: The dance of the Dards at Gilgit. Leitner sits on the verandah clapping his hands to the music. In his narrative he writes of spending his soirée clutching a pen in one hand and a pistol in the other

Below: The Kamri Pass on the road to Gilgit

customs dues. And a few apparently thought it was a portrait of the author. 'Dear me,' remarked one, 'what a very extraordinary looking man Mr Waterton must be.'

Undeterred the Squire now attempted further freaks. There was a whole gallery of anthropomorphic monsters which were meant to represent Protestant reformers. There was a ghastly 'Noctifer', a menacing blend of bittern and eagle-owl, and most alarming of all, at the foot of the stairs crouched the 'Nightmare'.

'This horrid incubus has a human face, grinning and displaying the frightfully formidable tusks of the wild boar, the hands of a man, satanic horns, elephant's ears, bat's wings, one cloven foot, the other that of an eagle widely expanding his terrific looking talons, and the tail of a serpent.'

No sinister purpose attached to these experiments. The Squire looked on them, as he looked on all creation, with benevolence and much humour. He relished surprise, and in old age gave free rein to his love of pranks. Visitors might find him lurking beneath the table and pretending to be a dog, or might be greeted by one of his slippers mischievously discharged in their direction. Aged seventy-seven he delighted a select audience by 'scratching the back part of his head with the big toe of his right foot'. Two years later he was seen to leap over a wire fence three and a half feet high. And at eighty he was still climbing trees. Falls seemed not to discourage him; but a week short of his eighty-third birthday he tripped on a briar and fell heavily on top of a log. He was conveyed back to the Hall in great pain. Priest, doctor and family assembled. The old wanderer knew he was dying. He blessed them all, received the last sacraments and recited the first verses of the *Dies Irae*.

'The end was now at hand [wrote one of those present], and he died at twenty-seven minutes past two in the morning of 27 May 1865. The window was open. The sky was beginning to grow grey, a few rooks had cawed, the swallows were twittering, the landrail was croaking from the ox-close, and a favourite cock, which he used to call his morning gun, leaped out from some hollies, and gave his accustomed crow.'

The funeral took place on June 3rd which would have been the Squire's eighty-third birthday. For his last resting place he had chosen a leafy corner of the estate at the far end of the lake, a favourite haunt of his beloved water birds. Hither coffin, mourners and celebrants proceeded in a procession of boats. The

Bishop of Beverley in mitre and robes with four canons and thirteen priests led the way in the first boat. To the dipping of oars they chanted the *Dies Irae* and the *De Profundis*. Behind came the coffin in the estate's coal boat and, after three boat-loads of mourners, the Squire's yacht, draped in black crepe, took up the rear. Other mourners lined the shore; the Misses Edmondstone paid their last respects from a nearby island. As the coffin was lowered into the grave a bird, this time unidentified, burst into song.

5
'That Sublime Vagabond'
Joseph Wolff

Invited to be a fly on the wall at just one historical encounter, the connoisseur of eccentric travellers would surely choose that summer's day in 1842 when the Squire of Walton Hall, Wakefield, entertained the Anglican curate of High Hoyland, Wakefield. By an extraordinary coincidence this corner of still rural England was then blessed not only with the ageing and engaging Charles Waterton but also with the impossible and irrepressible Joseph Wolff – and in spite of Waterton's notorious unsociability, they did indeed meet.

It was Wolff who saw to that. His stay at High Hoyland he deemed the happiest in his life. For the first time in thirty years he knew the joys of a home; his devoted wife could shower her attentions on him and their young son could begin his education. But Wolff was as naturally sociable as the Squire was not. For a man who had rubbed shoulders with popes and patriarchs, kings, amirs and emperors, Wakefield society left something to be desired. Specifically he longed for a good theological wrangle. What more natural than that he should seek out his most inter-esting neighbour, 'that great traveller and earnest and straight-forward Roman Catholic, Mr Waterton'?

A mere curate – and like all curates, chronically hard up – Wolff was innocent of any excessive presumption in this. As his pony and trap clattered over the drawbridge of Walton Hall the flat, pasty-faced visitor was as instantly recognisable as the crew-cut Squire. Wolff could already look back on twenty years of wanderings every bit as bizarre as his host's. He, too, was a celebrity and so, indeed, was his wife, a lady of the utmost consequence being the erstwhile Lady Georgiana Walpole, beauty of repute and grand-daughter of the Prime Minister.

The double doors of Walton Hall swung open and the Wolffs trooped in to whatever welcome the Squire had devised. Was Lady Georgiana, one wonders, grazed by a playfully thrown slipper? Or was their host hiding under the hall table doing one of his canine impersonations? Confronted by that ghastly 'Nightmare' at the foot of the staircase, Wolff would surely have declaimed a suitable text by way of an impromptu exorcism. Casting out devils was the one miracle he had successfully performed and Waterton, who liked nothing better than a good miracle, was doubtless delighted to hear how it was worked. He responded by confiding in Wolff a wondrous tale of St Alphonsius Maria Liguori who 'had been in two places at one and the same time'. He also let Wolff into the secret of the miraculous conversion of a Jew by the name of Ratisbon who was then preaching the Gospel in Jerusalem. Wolff found this fascinating. Ratisbon was only the second Jew to preach Christianity in Jerusalem since Christ; Wolff himself was the first.

Other gems which transpired at this meeting went unrecorded. Sadly Waterton never mentioned the visit and Wolff only recalled it twenty years after the event. The scope for conjecture is therefore considerable and the liveliest imagination might be sorely taxed in doing it justice. Waterton must soon have discovered that Wolff knew nothing about natural history just as Wolff would have found that Waterton was surprisingly indifferent to the brass tacks of scriptural criticism. But both men loved ecclesiastical gossip and even in matters of faith they were not as far apart as might have been expected. Wolff, though now a protégé of the Evangelical movement, retained a great affection for the Church of Rome. First loves are never forgotten; as the curate warmed to the subject of his long and chequered search for a congenial religious haven, his wild eyes would glaze over with a look of rapture. The voice wavered and the German accent became more pronounced. To one whose love of Christ had never faltered, there was no shame in having lived the life of a doctrinal Casanova.

It had all started in 1802 when Wolff underwent his first conversion. His father, a rabbi in Bavaria, had been fielding awkward questions ever since his first-born could talk. 'He is always walking about and thinking, which is not natural,' complained the rabbi. The young Wolff continued to walk about and think and, at the age of seven, inspired by his Protestant barber, he declared his firm conviction that the Messiah had already come – in the person of Jesus Christ. He ran to the nearest clergyman, a Lutheran, and asked to be received into the Christian Church. The Lutheran cautioned patience; but from then on the only question in Wolff's mind was which Christian persuasion to adopt.

Four years later attendance at a school in Bamberg gave him the opportunity of religious instruction as meted out by the Catholics.

The story of Paul's conversion and the lives of Francis Xavier and Ignatius Loyola became his new inspiration. With the wisdom of years – he was now eleven – he declared for Catholicism and resolved to be a Jesuit missionary. Moses Lazarus Cohen, the cousin with whom he was staying, thought this a great joke and was the first of many to call him an 'enthusiast', a word which then had connotations of mental derangement. Mrs Cohen was less amused.

'[She] became very angry and threw a poker at him [i.e. Wolff; like Waterton he preferred to speak of himself in the third person], and cursed him and turned him out of the house. Wolff left Bamberg without saying one word and without a single farthing in his pocket, and travelled towards Wurtzburg.'

Thus began the thirty years of wandering and seeking – or 'walking about and thinking' – which finally, by ways long and devious, brought him to the Yorkshire parish of High Hoyland. From Bamberg he went to Frankfurt, then Halle, Prague, Vienna, Pressburg, Munich, Saxe Weimar, Heidelberg, Soleure and back to Prague. His needs were few. Occasionally he taught Hebrew; more often he simply presented himself as an eager convert in need of instruction and shelter. Neither Protestant professors, rationalist philosophers nor Catholic abbots could refuse him. By the time he reached Prague in 1812 he had studied at no less than twelve different academies, lyceums, gymnasiums and monasteries. He had canvassed the merits of Christianity with prelates and scholars of every persuasion. And he was as determined as ever to become a Catholic missionary. He was baptised by the Benedictine abbot of Emaus and took the christian name of Joseph.

There then followed another four years of theological rambles in Central Europe. Even within the Catholic Church there were enough different schools of thought to keep the new convert in a turmoil of debate and constantly on the move. With a view to his future role as a missionary he was also studying oriental languages and brushing up his Hebrew by tackling a new translation of the Bible. This latter undertaking won him the patronage of Count Friedrich Stolberg, a poet and patriarch who was to exercise a great influence over Wolff. At Stolberg's home in Westphalia he glimpsed a new world of gracious living allied to a devout but liberal Catholicism. To a young vagabond who habitually mixed with religious firebrands this more tolerant and patrician version of Christianity made a deep appeal. The Count had eighteen children – 'sons like thunder and daughters like lightning'.

'It was delightful to look at this family when they rode out after dinner on horseback; and Wolff felt himself transported into the old times of knighthood when he saw the old count coming forth from the burgh with his thundering boys and chaste daughters.'

Wolff was enraptured. His own life would continue tempestuous and unsettled, his financial means would be negligible and even his appearance would be notoriously scruffy. But always he retained this vision of order, of family piety and aristocratic decorum; it explains his eventual rapport with the English aristocracy and indeed his marriage into it. Likewise Stolberg's religious views prepared him for Anglicanism. For though a respected Catholic, the Count did not hold with papal infallibility or with the worship of the Virgin Mary; he was even prepared to consider Luther a saint. This accorded closely with Wolff's own sympathies. In the happy belief that the Catholic Church welcomed such broadmindedness, he shouldered his knapsack and headed for Rome.

Rome was already aware of its ardent Jewish convert. Even the Pope was anxious to meet the new prodigy. 'You are my son,' declared Pius VII at their first audience, and Wolff, overcome by His Holiness' holiness, stooped to kiss his feet. A papal hand quickly intercepted; but Wolff's demonstrative nature was not easily baulked. Instead he 'gently and caressingly patted His Holiness on the shoulder saying "I love Your Holiness. Give me your blessing."'

'Then kneeling down he received the benediction of that holy man, of which he will always treasure the most pleasing recollection, in spite of those bigoted protestants who declare the Pope to be anti-Christ.'

Bigotry was not a prerogative of the Protestants. Even that familiar patting of the papal shoulder would get him into trouble. He had come to Rome to study for the priesthood and on Pius VII's personal recommendation he was admitted to the Collegio Romano. At the very first lecture he leapt to his feet to protest against some reference to papal infallibility. His fellow students were aghast; but in spite of official warnings, Wolff continued to regard the Pope as no more than an exalted prelate; he was certainly not God and it was blasphemous to treat him as such.

In representing the voice of dissent Wolff admitted that he often overstepped the mark:

'His [i.e. Wolff's] great enemies all through life have been vanity and ambition. He owns that during his life at Rome his vanity made him believe that he knew everything better than those by whom he was surrounded; and as people told him that he was like Luther in outward appearance, he resolved, if possible to be a Luther also in his stormy and wild career; while at the same time his insatiable ambition made him wish and aim at becoming pope, as he once openly avowed in the Collegio. And being then an admirer of Gregory VII, he said he wished to be like him in daring but to do exactly the contrary to what he did, and to signalise himself by abolishing celibacy and the worship of the saints. He even told his fellow pupils of the name he intended to assume when pope, namely Hildebrandus I.'

Far from Wolff accepting the tenets of the Church, the Church was expected to adopt the tenets of Wolff. This was not just ambition and vanity but rank heresy. The wonder is that he was not immediately expelled.

Expulsion, though, was always the only possible outcome. The Inquisition was still active, if not especially vigilant, and Wolff was positively daring it to act. One day in April 1818 a tailor, a shoe-maker and a hatter successively presented themselves at his room, silently took his measurements and went away. 'Wolff was in great apprehension and did not know what to do.' A few days later he was summoned before the Cardinal. A new suit of clothes awaited him as did a glass of Tokay, by way of refreshment, a dwarf, by way of jailor, twenty-five gendarmes and an officer of the Inquisition. Still uncertain whether he was destined for the stake, prison or exile, he was bundled aboard a carriage and 'thus rolled out of the Holy City'.

They headed for Venice and then, to his relief, for Vienna. It was exile. But apprehension only gave way to gloom and despondency. His great ambition to preach Christianity, especially to his Jewish brethren, had come to nothing. He was back where he started, still considering himself a Catholic but denied all chance of fulfilment within the Catholic Church. For a time he studied at a Redemptorist monastery in Switzerland and it was in Lausanne that, on an impulse, he stopped an English lady in the street. Did she, he enquired, by any chance know a Mr Henry Drummond of Drummond's Bank? Indeed she did and, 'like a flash of lightning', she asked if she had the honour to be addressing the 'Abbé Wolff'. By a happy coincidence she had been waiting for him. Henry Drummond, banker, philanthropist and religious entrepreneur, had befriended Wolff in Rome and, confidently expecting his disappointment there, had left word for anyone who met him to send him on to England. Miss Greaves, the lady in Lausanne, did just that; in 1819 Wolff landed at Dover.

Drummond had been fired by Wolff's zeal and aptitude for missionary work. He realised that the Teutonic obsession with theological niceties and the Roman insistence on dogma were side-tracking his energies. What Wolff needed was not a Church but a patron – a role which Drummond was keen to fill. Arrived in London, Wolff understood that his choice of Church was as irrelevant as the cut of his coat. Drummond kindly took him on an ecclesiastical shopping spree. They tried the Baptists, the Quakers and then the Methodists before Wolff sensibly opted for the Church of England as alone offering the doctrinal capacity which could accommodate his particular anatomy of beliefs. An added incentive was that the Church of England boasted a 'Society for Promoting Christianity amongst the Jews'. Drummond again performed the introduction and Wolff was soon despatched to Cambridge under the auspices of the Society to study divinity and oriental languages.

Two years later, in 1821, he sailed for the Mediterranean with a trunk full of Bibles to begin the conversion of the Jews. His predecessors from the Society had been a bitter disappointment. One had become a Mohammedan, another a thief, a third a pick-pocket and the fourth a mercenary. Wolff was determined to do better and at first valiantly confined his activities to the large Jewish communities of the eastern Mediterranean. Between Cairo and Antioch there was scarcely a town in which he did not proclaim his conversion and argue the merits of Christianity. But converts proved hard to come by. He suspected he would do better amongst the smaller, less sophisticated Jewish communities scattered through Mesopotamia, Persia and Central Asia. He was also keen to preach not only to the Jews but to members of the various Orthodox churches and even to the Mohammedans – all of which amounted to a splendid pretext for widening the scope of his mission indefinitely. Without waiting for approval, he embarked on what would become a world-wide reconnaissance for the prospects of Christian endeavour.

During the 1820s he veered east as far as Baghdad and Teheran and then swept north through the Caucasus, the Crimea and Constantinople. This was as nothing to what followed. In 1830 he was back in the Mediterranean contemplating a plunge into the Sahara to Timbuktu. Then he suddenly changed his mind and headed east again. He crossed Persia, reached the forbidden city of Bukhara in Central Asia, wandered through Afghanistan, set off across the Himalayas and, turning back, finally travelled the length of India to Cochin and then back to Bombay. Additionally he toured in America and made short forays to Ireland, Abyssinia and the Yemen. Wolff believed that conversion was a matter for divine inspiration and not the product of laborious instruction. He invoked the example of St Paul, his favourite saint, and no doubt recalled his own impulsive changes of faith. A sermon, a proclamation, a debate, a prayer – it was enough just to sow the seed. He founded no schools, he collected no disciples, and he rarely stayed anywhere longer than a week. People did indeed remember the man – who could forget a wild-eyed, flaxen-haired, and absent-minded Jew, with several camel loads of Bibles, who regarded his conversion as a passport to the indulgence of society in four continents? They admired his sincerity, they enjoyed his absurdity, and they could – and frequently did – punish his impudence. But few, very few, responded to his call.

Back in London the Society for Promoting Christianity amongst the Jews was far from happy about the turn of events. They remonstrated against what was becoming too personal a crusade, they tried to recall him, and they eventually disowned him. But not before the Reverend Lewis Way, director of the Society, had tracked him down. Way was the man responsible for recruiting Wolff. He was loth indeed to desert him and in making a case for their erratic emissary he brilliantly captured the essence of Wolff's achievement.

'Wolff is so extraordinary a creature, there is no calculating *a priori* concerning his motions. He appears to me to be a comet without any perihelion, and capable of setting a whole system on fire. When I should have addressed him in Syria, I heard of him in Malta; and when I supposed him gone to England, he was riding like a ruling angel in the whirlwinds of Antioch or standing unappalled amongst the crumbling towers of Aleppo. A man who at Rome calls the Pope "the dust of the earth" and tells the Jews at Jerusalem that "the Gemara is a lie"; who passes his days in disputation and his nights in digging the *Talmud*; to whom a floor of brick is a feather bed and a box a bolster; who makes, or finds, a friend alike in the persecutor of his former or present faith; who can conciliate a Pasha or confute a Patriarch; who travels without a guide; speaks without an interpreter; can live without food and pay without money; forgiving all the insults he meets with and forgetting all the flattery he receives; who knows little of worldly conduct and yet accommodates himself to all men without giving offence to any – such a man (and such and more is Wolff) must excite no ordinary degree of attention in a country and among a people whose monotony of manners and habits has remained undisturbed for centuries.

'As a pioneer I deem him matchless . . . but if order is to be established or arrangements made, trouble not Wolff. He knows of no church but his heart; no calling but that of zeal; no dispensation but that of preaching. He is devoid of enmity towards man and full of the love of God. By such an instrument, whom no school has taught, whom no college could hold, is the way of the Judaean wilderness preparing. This is Providence, showing the nothingness of the wisdom of the wise and bringing to nothing the understanding of the prudent. Thus are his brethren provoked to emulation and stirred up to enquiry. They all perceive – as everyone must – that whatever he is, he is in earnest; they acknowledge him to be a sincere believer in Jesus of Nazareth; and that is a great point gained with them.'

The only thing which Way overlooked was the appalling danger to which Wolff was constantly exposed. He was safe enough with Jews and Brahmins and he came to look on the Eastern Christians – Nestorians, Copts, Jacobites, Chaldaeans, Sabeans, Armenians and Syrians – as his particular friends. But when he provoked disputes with orthodox Sunni Mohammedans, Persian Sufis or devil-worshipping Yezidis, he was asking for trouble. Most of the more martial tribes of Asia – Bedouins, Kurds, Wahabis, Turkomans and Hazaras – could claim to have made him their prisoner at least once and he was attacked and robbed more times than can be counted. Other risks of the trade included a bastinado near Baghdad, a poisoning attempt in Jerusalem, being dragged across the desert of Khorassan tied to a horse's tail, and being left to cross the snowy Hindu Kush stark naked. Then there were the natural hazards. He caught dysentery in Cairo, typhus in Tiflis and cholera in Hyderabad, he coincided with the earthquake that flattened Aleppo and – a serious business for a non-swimmer – was shipwrecked in both the Mediterranean and the Black Sea.

Wolff was no hero and in relating these hair-breadth escapes he made no attempt to disguise his panic. It was this combination of human frailty and super-human endurance which, more even than his missionary work, endeared him to the general public – that and of course his improbable marriage. As with all Wolff's major decisions, matrimony was the product of impulse. Arriving back in London for a flying visit in 1826, he found a dinner invitation awaiting him for that very evening. Amongst the guests paraded to inspect the returning prodigy he instantly recognised 'his darling angel in earthly shape'. Pleasantly handsome, of independent means and impeccably connected, Lady Georgiana Walpole was highly eligible. Wolff, on the other hand, was not. Obscure origins, gauche – even gross – habits, disastrous looks, financial incompetence and a bizarre vocation – not to mention his questionable sanity – should have guaranteed him a lifetime of bachelorhood. Yet within six months he had married. Never was there a more ill-assorted couple, and never was there a happier one. Together they returned to the Mediterranean and, in between Lady Georgiana's confinements, together they shared the trials and tribulations of the missionary life.

'On the ninth day of this journey [from Cairo to Jerusalem] Lady Georgiana tried dromedary riding which she much preferred to the camel. She described it as only requiring the use of stirrups to make it exceedingly comfortable.'

She did not, however, accompany him to India. By then their first child had tragically died in Cyprus and their second, Henry Drummond Wolff, was still a babe in arms. Wolff went alone and for once felt the pangs of separation. In 1838 he willingly abjured further wanderings in favour of domesticity. He had already become a naturalised British subject. He now identified further with the land of his adoption by being ordained into the Church of England. Hence his appointment to the curacy of the little parish of High Hoyland in the county of Yorkshire.

In 1842, the year he met Waterton, Wolff was forty-seven years old. He was justly famous, grossly overweight and blissfully happy. All he needed was a slightly more remunerative appointment and, as he confided to Waterton, this was imminent. He had been offered the job of Anglican chaplain in the city of Bruges. After fond farewells to their parishioners the Wolffs headed south to spend a few weeks in London before crossing to Belgium.

In London Wolff should have been in his element, renewing old acquaintances and parading his family. In fact he was in a fever of anticipation. Five thousand miles away in the heart of Central Asia two British officers were being held hostage by a capricious and fanatical Amir. They had been tortured and they might well now be dead. One of them, Captain Arthur Conolly, Wolff had actually met in India. But that was beside the point. The point was that they were in Bukhara and the only other Englishman alive who had ever entered that city was Wolff. He knew the awesome Amir, he knew the lawless Turkoman tribes whose desert raiding accounted for Bukhara's isolation, and he knew that it was his duty to step forward and be counted.

In a letter to the *Morning Herald* he did just that. It was addressed to 'all the Officers of the British Army' and proffered his services to go and rescue the hostages provided someone would pay his expenses. He was confident he could reach Bukhara and confident that the hostages were still alive. 'I merely want the expense of my journey and not one single farthing as compensation.' As he saw it, he would simply be settling an old debt. He owed everything to his adopted country and in particular to its serving officers. In the remotest corners of Asia the timely intervention of a passing major or colonel had so often restored him to health or happiness that he had come to look on the British army as 'sent to me by God'. In 1821, robbed on the road from Gaza, a Major Mackworth had come to his rescue. In 1823 it was the turn of Colonel The Hon. Hobart Cradock to 'nurse him like a brother' when he was taken sick in Jerusalem. 1824 was the year of his Baghdad bastinado; Colonel The Hon. George Keppel and friends materialised from nowhere with money and medical aid. The next year he lay unconscious beside a road in the Caucasus with the Tiflis typhus when Colonel Sir James Russel came driving by; he was scooped into the carriage and borne away to the nearest sanatorium. 1826 was a blank, but in 1827 he scrambled ashore in Cephalonia after his first shipwreck to be greeted by Colonel (later General Sir) Charles Napier. ('The first thing that extraordinary man said was "I know your sister-in-law, Lady Catherine Long, very well. She is one of the prettiest women I ever saw"'.) 1829, Cairo and that case of dysentery; Lord Prudhoe – later the Duke of Northumberland – and a Colonel Felix 'showed him the greatest kindness'. And so on. Perhaps the most remarkable coincidence had come in Afghanistan in 1832. After being waylaid, all but martyred (or rather 'made into sausages'), and then obliged to brave the blizzards of the Hindu Kush without a stitch of clothing, he approached Kabul shivering and destitute. At the time no British officer had ever been near the place; but he was in dire straits. He prayed exceptionally hard. Sure enough Lieutenant (later Colonel Sir) Alexander Burnes and companions reached the city that very night. He was saved once again.

Now it was his turn to play guardian angel. The Foreign Office tried to discourage him; even Lady Georgiana 'felt reluctant to my encountering the matter'. But a Captain Grover read his letter in the *Morning Herald* with interest and undertook to raise a public subscription. Grover had originally offered to go himself, only standing down when he was refused permission to wear uniform. Wolff took an equal pride in his canonicals and, by way of a snub to the Foreign Office, insisted that he would never change until the job was done.

'[Wolff decided] he would embark from Southampton dressed in his clergyman's gown, doctor's hood [he was a Doctor of Divinity and proud of it] and shovel hat, with a Bible in Hebrew and English (Baxter's edition) in his hand. He would assume the title of "Joseph Wolff, the Grand Dervish of England, Scotland and Ireland, and of the whole of Europe and America", and he would demand the bodies, either dead or alive, of Colonel Stoddart and Captain Conolly when he reached Bukhara.'

Brave words, but the Grand Dervish was also taking all reasonable precautions. The Foreign Office reluctantly agreed to commend his mission to its scattered representatives, especially the British ministers in Constantinople and Teheran. Meanwhile Grover was having considerable success in rousing the nation's conscience. Lord Melbourne, the ex-Prime Minister, was one of the appeal's principal subscribers; Admiral Codrington, the victor of the battle of Navarino, was on the rescue committee; and the P & O Line chipped in with a free passage to Constantinople. The thing was gaining momentum fast. In mid-September Wolff sent Grover a list of his travelling requirements:

'1 I shall take with me a clergyman's gown and cassock, my hood, and a shovel hat.

'2 One dozen or two of Hebrew Bibles and Testaments and of the Common Prayer book in Hebrew for the Jews of Bukhara, Shahr Sabz, Khiva, Samarkand, Balkh and Khokand. These you may get from the London Society for Promoting Christianity amongst the Jews.

'3 Two or three dozens of silver watches for the Grand Mullah and mullahs of Bukhara, the khans of Khiva, Shahr Sabz and Khokand. The Amir of Bukhara shall not get one single thing in case he was the cause of their [the hostages'] deaths.

'4 Two or three dozens of maps in Arabic characters, published by the Church Missionary Society.

'5 Three dozens of *Robinson Crusoe*, translated into Arabic by Mr Schlienz of Malta. I distributed a great many copies of this book when at Sana'a and Luhaiya in Arabia and I assure you it excited a great sensation. Robinson Crusoe's adventures and wisdom were read in the market places of Sana'a, Hodeida and Luhaiya and admired and believed.'

On 14 October 1843 he arrived in Southampton and boarded the *Iberia*. A substantial crowd of well-wishers had gathered, but according to Grover, 'there was no weeping or wailing'; he might just as well have been 'taking a trip to the Isle of Wight'. Lady Georgiana and young Henry Drummond Wolff made their solemn farewells; 'they knew he was performing a sacred duty'. Wolff blessed them all and gave Grover a parting hug and a kiss. The ship sailed slowly away.

Wolff turned from the railings and addressed himself to the business in hand. His fellow passengers quickly succumbed to sea-sickness. Not so Wolff. The experienced traveller knew how to deal with these things. Hatless, he paced the deck in the bracing air, slept on a sofa in the dining-room rather than in his claustrophobic berth, and had buckets of sea water poured over him every morning.

'We made nine miles an hour and arrived off Ushant on the 15th. I wrote to my dear wife and son to beg them to pray for me and that, by the Lord's will, I trusted that we should soon again be united and live happily together in God – that Christ who, after all he had done in nineteen centuries, was still expected, since as yet the heathen are not given to him for his inheritance nor the utmost parts of the earth for his possession.'

The utmost parts of the earth included Bukhara. He was here alluding to his deepest and most controversial conviction – that the Second Coming, to be followed by the Personal Reign of Christ, was imminent. A fundamentalist where scripture was concerned, Wolff believed in miracles (he had, after all, performed one) and in visions (he had had several, including one with Christ in Kabul and a particularly impressive encounter with St Paul and the Heavenly host in Malta). If the Bible was right about miracles and visions, then it must also be right about the Second Coming. By careful observation of natural disasters, etc., and by laborious calculation, he had earlier convinced himself that this was due in 1847. Now, with only four years to go and still no obvious candidate for the role of Anti-Christ, he was beginning to doubt his arithmetic. But the end was still, unquestionably, nigh. He had been labouring the point for twenty years and he continued to do so on board the *Iberia* once his captive congregation had emerged from their sick-beds.

'On Monday the 17th I gave a lecture to the ship's company and at 6 p.m. we passed Cape Finisterre. On Tuesday the 18th I lectured again. We had then Cape St Vincent in sight. On the 19th, when off Cadiz, I continued my lecture. On the 20th early in the morning we entered Gibraltar . . .

'On the 21st of October I continued my lectures to the passengers; Sunday the 22nd I read divine service and preached; Monday the 23rd I lectured again. Tuesday the 24th we were off Tunis; Wednesday the 25th we sailed with contrary wind and passed early in the morning the island of Zemra. I had a conversation with several passengers on the necessity of faith and obedience and on the Personal Reign of Christ and the Restoration of the Jews.'

Next day they reached Malta and, three days later, Piraeus. Wolff dashed off to Athens for a day's sight-seeing. He climbed the Acropolis and proclaimed chapter XVII of the Acts of the Apostles from the Areopagus. He spent the night with the English chaplain, breakfasted with the British Ambassador, and then had an audience with King Otho and his Queen. The King was interested in the state of the Armenian Church; Wolff enlightened him. The Queen turned out to be a niece of his old patron Count Friedrich Stolberg. 'She is really a most beautiful and lovely Queen – the very *beau ideal* of a Queen,' thought the Doctor; she even took off her glove when he stooped to kiss her hand.

'What travels you have undertaken,' declared the fair Queen. 'What extraordinary travels.'

'In order to obtain a great object, one must make great exertions,' explained Wolff with untypical sanctimony.

In the afternoon he called on the President of the Greek Synod, Bishop Neophitos, then hastened back to Piraeus. Alas, too late; the *Iberia* had already sailed. But all was not lost. The British navy was in port and, on Wolff's plight becoming known, Captain Sir James Stirling rose from the dinner table and the SS *Vesuvius* was ordered to sea. They overhauled the *Iberia* at Syra; 'I was hailed with cheers by the whole ship's company.' Even the fat Methodist lady who, from the security of her husband's lap, habitually interrupted his lectures joined in the welcome.

The next stop was Constantinople. Here Wolff left the *Iberia* and spent three frantic weeks preaching and doing the diplomatic rounds. Count Titov, the Russian Ambassador, informed him that the Tsar had sent special orders to his Governors in Siberia and to his admirals on the Caspian sea; should Wolff strike Russian territory anywhere between Astrakhan and Irkutsk he was assured of a warm welcome. The French and Italian Ambassadors had him to dinner as did Count Sturmer, the Austrian Internuncio; after dinner the Count was rewarded with an eight-part lecture in German on the Second Coming. This same lecture, only in English, was also delivered at the home of Sir Stratford Canning, the British Minister. In the Cannings Wolff found his kindest and most enthusiastic supporters. Sir Stratford helped obtain letters of introduction from the Sultan, his Foreign Minister, and the highest Islamic officials addressed to all the khans, amirs and mullahs of Central Asia. In the absence of any such letters from the British Government, Wolff set great store by these missives and got Lady Canning herself to stitch them into the lining of his coat. She also provided a good stock of tea and sugar. Then, after protracted farewells and good wishes, a steamer bound for Trebizond at the far end of the Black Sea bore him away. The journey, which to date had been more like a royal progress, was about to begin in earnest.

Perusing the ship's visitors book Wolff noticed the signature of Arthur Conolly. He had sailed this way in 1839. 'Poor man,' exclaimed the Doctor, 'dear good man, for Wolff loved him very much.' Whether or not he and Stoddart were still alive remained one of the great imponderables of the mission. The last letters from the hostages, smuggled out of Bukhara in the previous year, had been filled with dire forebodings. Stoddart had served a long spell in the notorious Black Well, a deep pit swarming with vermin, reptiles and insects which had been specially bred to prey upon the victims. Both men had been ill and both had been obliged to wear the same clothes for more than three months. The Amir they described as a monster of evil who was keeping them alive only as long as it amused him to do so.

According to reports reaching Teheran, he had ceased to be amused nearly eighteen months before Wolff set off. But although the British Government had accepted these reports and listed the men as dead, there had been persistent rumours to the contrary. In Constantinople Wolff had heard more reports from Bukhara and still they conflicted. For the eternal optimist there were yet grounds for hope. Besides, Wolff found it hard to believe that the Amir could be so inhuman. Like the two or three other travellers who had reached the forbidden city in the nineteenth century, he had had no reason to complain of the Amir Nasrullah.

At Trebizond there were more rumours that the hostages might yet be alive. Wolff paused only to lecture the small expatriate community – this time in Italian – and collect the £44 raised towards his expenses; he had not yet had to touch the £500 raised by Grover.

'I set out on December 1st for Erzerum with my Serbian servant Michael, a Tatar of the Pasha [of Trebizond], and an excellent Turk who always walked near me when I ascended the precipices of Trebizond. The road from Trebizond to Erzerum was horrid, so that I walked the whole way on foot.'

Wolff was a deplorable horseman and usually preferred walking. But this was December and they were climbing into the Anatolian mountains. The snow drifts were neck deep. Even for the Tartar and the excellent Turk, manhandling the Doctor in such conditions was a two-man job. To their relief the mission ground to a halt in Erzerum. Blizzards raged and from the road ahead exposure victims were daily being brought into town. Reluctantly Wolff stayed put.

As luck would have it, Erzerum's foreign community happened to be swelled by the presence of a boundary commission, including several British officers. They, as of old, rallied to his aid. In particular there was Colonel William Fenwick Williams. He insisted that henceforth Wolff would only be safe in the snow if he rode. Accordingly he provided an outfit which was supposed to ensure the rider against frostbite. Besides three or four layers of padded coats and trousers, it included boots which reached to his hips 'like the horseguards', and an immense wolf-skin coat and hood; 'thus I was a Wolff in wolf's clothing'. (But did the doctoral hood and shovel hat fit inside the fur hat?) The Colonel also gave him the rare satisfaction of baptising a Jew. This was the Colonel's servant, a young man 'of the most excellent character' who went by the unlikely name of Friday. Presumably the Colonel was also a *Robinson Crusoe* fan.

Christmas came and still the blizzards blew. Wolff preached and consoled himself by issuing proclamations. One was to the entire Armenian nation asking them to use whatever contacts they might have in Bukhara on his behalf. The other was even more general being designed to circulate amongst all the Mohammedans of Central Asia.

FOLLOWERS OF ISLAM!

In the whole Turkish empire, Arabia and Afghanistan, you remember me well. I have been among you at Damascus, Egypt,

Aleppo, Baghdad, Isfahan, Bukhara, Kabul and Hindustan [India]. I have conversed on the coming of Jesus Christ with Mohammedans, Jews, Parsees and Hindus. I have been well received, though differing in religious beliefs, by the Grand Moghul of Delhi and the Shah of Persia, the Grand Mullahs of Baghdad, Constantinople, Isfahan, Kashmir and Bukhara. I have been to the utmost boundaries of the earth, even to America which is situated on the other side of the ocean. . . . Having learnt that two British officers of high merit have been put to death by order of the Amir of Bukhara I am going to Great Bukhara to ascertain the truth of that report; for I cannot believe it as I was well received at Bukhara and with great hospitality. . . . I call now on all Mohammedan princes and mullahs throughout the world to send letters of recommendation on my part to the King of Bukhara that he may receive me well.

Joseph Wolff.

At last, on December 27th, the weather lifted. Colonel Williams rode the first six miles with him and in the snow they toasted success with a bottle of Tenedos wine. Then the Grand Dervish rode clumsily off in the direction of Mount Ararat. He was now entering the Persian province of Azerbaijan whose capital, Tabriz, was his next port of call. Dodging blizzards and avalanches he descended towards the desert. The cold did not abate; Tabriz has a truly continental climate, dry and unbearably hot in the summer, and dry and unbearably cold in the winter. But nothing could have been warmer than the welcome of Mr Bonham, Her Majesty's Consul in Tabriz. Wolff baptised the Bonham child and was delighted to learn that Mrs Bonham was a niece of Sir Robert Peel. Altogether an excellent family, thought Wolff; but surely they deserved better than the Consul-Generalship of Tabriz. 'Why is Mr Bonham not made an ambassador?' he demanded of the influential rescue committee in London.

Through the good offices of Bonham he was enabled to pay a visit to the Tabriz gaol where languished Mohammed Khan Kerahe, alias 'The Head-tearer'. This was the man before whom Wolff had been dragged by Turkoman slave dealers after being towed across the desert tied to the tail of one of their horses. It had happened in Khorassan, on the other side of Persia, twelve years before but the Khan's reputation, like Wolff's, had not diminished.

'This fellow had put out the eyes of hundreds of people and cut off noses etc. and sold not less than sixty thousand Persians to the people of Bukhara. He may be compared with the Wild Boar of the Ardennes in *Quentin Durward*. His own turn, however, came; and as I like to see people in misfortune, not to triumph over them but to console them, I went to pay him a visit. . . . On my seeing him he immediately recognised me, reminded me of the bastinadoes he had inflicted on those who made me a slave and took my money; – but he prudently omitted to state that he put this latter commodity into his own pocket; and as Orientals have long recollections – and one may meet with them in out-place regions and rather unexpec-tedly – I omitted to revive any unpleasant reminiscences. By one of those freaks of physiognomy which occasionally happen, his appearance is remarkably mild; but I should shun that eye if I met it in the desert.'

Wolff contented himself with taking the man's autograph and making a copy of his genealogy; unsurprisingly he turned out to be a direct descendant of Genghiz Khan.

After this reminder of the lawless conditions that prevailed on Persia's north-eastern frontier, the onward journey to Teheran was comparatively uneventful. Michael, the Serbian servant, got drunk, knocked his master down, and later explained that he would be obliged to behave in exactly the same way whenever a feast day of the Virgin Mary called for celebration. Wolff sensibly dismissed him. The Doctor had never been much of a judge of character; on previous journeys his servants had included a thief, two drunkards, and an epileptic Negro.

In Teheran the British Ambassador was Colonel Justin Sheil, a quiet Roman Catholic and probably the only British officer about whom Wolff had reservations. It was Sheil who had evaluated and accepted the reports that the hostages were dead. He still believed them and he clearly regarded the Doctor's mission as an unneces-sary and potentially embarrassing stunt. For his part, Wolff con-tinued to insist that even in Teheran nothing was known for certain. But, twenty years later in his autobiography, he told a rather different story:

'And now Wolff at this moment makes a confession which he had never made before – that he himself had already, when at Teheran, the firmest conviction that neither Stoddart nor Conolly were in the land of the living in Bukhara, and that they had been put to death. But he withheld this conviction because he was afraid that if he was to return, acting upon this conviction, every one would say that the whole of his attempt to go to Bukhara had been a piece of humbug and was the work of a braggart. Wolff therefore concealed his internal conviction . . .'

However this may be, from Teheran onwards the anxieties of the Doctor, of Sheil, of the committee in London, and of the public at large centred less on the fate of the hostages and more on that of their would-be rescuer. Wolff himself now had a much clearer idea of the risks he ran. Stoddart and Conolly had incurred the Amir's wrath because they failed to produce letters of accreditation from Queen Victoria; Wolff did not even have letters from the Foreign Office, let alone the Queen. And again, if the hostages had been killed, the Amir was obviously trying to hide the fact; anyone coming to investigate it was simply inviting the same fate. Colonel Sheil, who would be Wolff's lifeline with the outside world, was unsympathetic; but there was no doubting his assessment of the situation and this was pessimistic in the extreme. He introduced Wolff to the Shah of Persia and the Shah, like the Sultan, wrote to Bukhara on his behalf. He also agreed to hold the Bukharan Ambassador in Teheran as a hostage for Wolff's safety. Both these seemed excellent ideas. But they supposed a degree of trust and friendship between Teheran and Bukhara that did not exist. Bukhara was a law unto itself and Amir Nasrullah answered to no man.

From being almost a royal progress, and then a diverting travel odyssey, the mission now became a grim piece of personal bravado. After Teheran there were no more glimpses of civilisation, no more of those genial British consuls, gallant officers and hospitable Eastern Christians, only deserts made perilous by the slave raiding Turkomans and, at the end, the most xenophobic and fanatical city in Central Asia. In Meshed, his last stop in Persia, Wolff found that even the small Jewish community had recently bowed to an age-old pressure and adopted Islam.

But on the credit side, the ever optimistic traveller thought he could detect 'a strong prestige rising in my favour'. From Meshed he loosed another salvo of letters to all the neighbouring powers urging them to use whatever influence they had at Bukhara on his behalf. The Governor of Meshed also promised his full support and appeared to have considerable influence over his Turkoman neighbours. These lords of the desert were still, in Wolff's opinion, 'a people of such a perfidious disposition and of such rapacity that one could not depend for a moment on their promises or treaties'. But the Governor was probably right when he advised that it was better to hunt with the hounds than run with the hare.

'"You go to the dangerous town of Bukhara," said the Governor. "There are about fifty thousand Mervi [Turkomans of Merv], the worst of people but very rich and of great influence with the Amir of Bukhara. And if one goes among rascals one must take a greater rascal to protect one. I shall therefore send with you nine rascals of the Mervi tribe; and if they don't behave well I will burn their wives and children who remain in my hands."

'Wolff then bethought himself, "I am in their hands and I must do what the Governor says; therefore I will take with me those nine rascals."'

On 31 March 1844, six months and five thousand miles after sailing from Southampton, he left Meshed and turned north for Bukhara. For the remaining five hundred miles he would travel with a caravan, sleeping in the desert at night and riding a camel by day. Food and water were scarce. His companions lived up to their reputation, constantly demanding presents and gleefully reminding him of the perils that lay in store at journey's end. At Merv he was delighted to find that the Turkoman *khalifa*, or religious leader, still remembered him from twelve years before. The old man emerged from his tent 'with bread and lemonade' and greeted him as a fellow dervish. But, alas, he too declared that the hostages were dead and that Wolff himself would share the same fate if he proceeded. 'To Bukhara I must go,' insisted Wolff, although now only too well aware that he would be placing himself 'in the hands of a despotic monarch of more than ordinary cruelty even for an Eastern dynasty'. 'Anticipating the worst,' he committed himself to divine providence and wrote to Lady Georgiana.

'My Dearest and Most Beloved Georgiana,
I set out after two hours from here to Bukhara. The *khalifa* of Merv has behaved most excellently towards me; he has sent one of his own disciples with me to Bukhara. Be of good spirits, my dearest Georgiana, for all that may happen to me here is of God. I go there *without much apprehension*. I often think of you and dear Henry, and pray pardon me, both of you, if I have ever uttered an unkind word. I love both of you more than myself. All the Turkomans behave very respectfully to me.
Your most loving husband,
Joseph Wolff.'

He also wrote to Grover urging that if the hostages were dead and that if he himself were to be martyred, something might yet be done for the two hundred thousand Persians who were held as slaves in Bukhara. Another letter, addressed to 'The Philanthropists of Europe', made the same plea. Surely, he seemed to be saying, *some* good must come from his efforts.

From Merv across the Oxus and over the last stretch of desert before the green fields of the Bukharan oases, Wolff walked, his cassock dragging in the sand and his faded shovel hat warding off sunstroke. In Turkey he had recited the German poems of his friend Count Stolberg as he waded through the snow-drifts. Now he read aloud from a Bible which he held before him. One by one his companions deserted, fearful of being seen to belong to such an ill-starred traveller. But the Christian dervish plodded on, defiantly proclaiming the word of God as if to ward off evil and exorcise the approaching city. 'I felt my power was in the Book and that its might would sustain me,' he wrote.

'The uncommon character of these proceedings attracted crowds from Shah Islam to Bukhara, all which was favourable to me – since if I was doomed to death, it would be widely known; and the consequences might seem serious to the Amir himself if he interfered with a sacred character, armed with the book of Moses, David and Jesus, protected by the word of the Khalifa of Merv, supported by the Sultan, the Shah of Persia, the Russian Ambassador and the Governor of Meshed.'

If ostentation was to be the key to survival, Wolff would not be found lacking. By the time he reached the city the entire population had got wind of the *feringhi* phenomenon that was bearing down on them. They thronged the streets and crammed the flat roof-tops. When the Grand Dervish appeared in his full canonicals with the doctoral hood of scarlet silk and the little black book, they bellowed an appreciative 'Salaam Aleikum'. 'Certainly twenty thousand people were in the streets shouting "Welcome, heartily welcome"'. Bukhara lay at the cross-roads of Asia's great trade routes; the throng included Uzbegs, Kirghiz, Kazakhs and Afghans, Sindis from India, Tartars from Russia and Tunganis from China; surely his triumphal entry would soon be noised from Constantinople to Calcutta and Canton.

Even the Amir was somewhat taken aback. Stoddart's troubles had apparently begun when he refused to make the customary obeisances. Wolff had no such scruples. He gravely stroked his beard and shouted 'Asylum of the World, Peace to the King'. He did it the usual three times and he continued doing it. He was approaching the thirtieth by the time the Amir's evil countenance dissolved.

'Enough, enough,' he said, and he mumbled something which

Wolff translated as 'Thou eccentric man, thou star with a tail, neither like a Jew nor a Christian nor a Hindu, nor a Russian nor an Uzbeg – so thou art Joseph Wolff'.

It seemed a propitious beginning. Wolff resolved to get at the truth while the Amir was disposed in his favour. Entering the city he had scanned the crowds hoping to recognise Stoddart and Conolly. 'It was in vain.' Now he came straight to the point. The whole world was waiting to hear; what had become of the two British officers? As if relieved to dispose of such a minor detail, the Amir flatly stated that he had executed them. Stoddart 'had not paid him the proper respect' and Conolly 'had a long nose (i.e was very proud)'.

The Doctor could never really make up his mind about Amir Nasrullah. On the one hand he was a cruel and autocratic tyrant who had murdered his way to power and who continued to sustain his authority by a rule of terror. In sudden bursts of temper his whole frame would go into convulsions and at such times he was 'as disagreeable a fellow as Wolff ever saw'. Against this, though, he was invariably solicitous for his poorer subjects, was indifferent to bribery, and was genuinely concerned when Wolff at last convinced him of the international outcry his actions had occasioned. For three days he sat lost in thought with his head in his hands. 'How extraordinary,' he told one of his advisers, 'I have two hundred thousand Persian slaves here and nobody comes for them. But on account of two Englishmen a person comes from England and single-handed demands their release.' In a fit of remorse he enquired whether, by any chance, the Christian dervish could bring them back to life. He clearly wanted to improve relations with Britain and he welcomed Wolff's quite unauthorised invitation to send an ambassador back to London with him.

The trouble was that, like many a tyrant, Nasrullah was intensely suspicious. During the weeks that followed, Wolff was repeatedly interrogated by his officers. News that his own Ambassador in Teheran was being held as a guarantee for Wolff's safety convinced him that the dervish must have some political standing. Yet, when asked to name the 'four Grand Viziers' and 'the twelve little viziers of England', Wolff gave a completely different list to that given by Stoddart and Conolly. Wolff tried to explain that the Cabinet had changed since 1841 and he ventured on a description of the workings of a democracy. 'But he made in that attempt such a hotch-potch that neither the King nor he himself could understand it.'

If Nasrullah was to some extent the victim of his own limited notions of kingship, no such excuse could be made for one of his principal advisers. This was Abdul Samut Khan, known as the Naib. Wolff, like Stoddart and Conolly, was befriended by this man and accepted his hospitality as a refuge from the unpredictable Amir. The Naib gave him the full story of the hostages' deaths and Wolff wrote to Grover to report that the mystery was cleared up and that he was about to leave for home. This was in early May. Three times his departure date was set and three times it passed without his being released. 'I soon found out that I was surrounded by a mass of treachery nearly unparalleled.'

Nasrullah kept demanding more and more irrelevant information. Why were there no camels in England? ('I had to write an immense time before he comprehended our railroad travelling.') Why did the Queen not execute more people? Did the English practise witchcraft? And how many farsakhs an hour could a steamship go? He was also beginning to enjoy Wolff's growing sense of gloom. A request for the bones of Stoddart and Conolly was met with the reply that the only bones that would be going to England were those of Wolff himself. Meanwhile the Naib's true colours were being revealed. The price of his friendship was money and when Wolff's credit ran out, so did the Naib's hospitality. Worse still, he admitted that it was he who had instigated the Amir to dispose of the hostages.

Wolff finally lost patience, had a blazing row with the Naib, and made an abortive attempt to escape. He was removed to the house in which Stoddart and Conolly had spent their last days. June gave way to July, the temperature soared and Wolff tried to cheer himself by singing German *lieder* at the top of his voice. The Amir cold-shouldered him and then departed on a campaign. His guards and servants gloated as each new rumour confirmed his imminent plight. The Naib was now actively canvassing his execution. His health was deteriorating, his confidence was shattered, and all hope of escaping faded. 'What I suffered all the time of the King's absence I cannot describe.' To ward off despair he wrote a last letter to Lady Georgiana.

'My dearest Wife and Child,

Never, never for a moment lose your love and obedience and faith in Jesus Christ; and pray for me that I may remain faithful to him in the hour of trial. Entreat the churches in England to pray for me to our blessed Redeemer, Jesus Christ. Give my regards to all my friends.

Your most loving Husband and Father,
Joseph Wolff.'

Next day a mullah came to him to demand that he turn Mohamme-dan. 'Never, never, never,' he replied. The mullah went away and his place was taken by the executioner, 'the same man who had put to death both Stoddart and Conolly'. He had come to inspect his next victim, he explained.

'I prepared for death and carried opium about with me that, in case my throat should be cut, I might not feel pain. However, at last I cast away the opium and prayed and wrote in my Bible these words.

"My dearest Georgiana and Henry,
I have loved both of you unto death,
Your affectionate husband and father, J. Wolff."'

Faced with death he clearly experienced both a crisis of faith and of heart. Later he would be accused of exaggerating his peril; but his journal admits of no such interpretation. He was scared stiff and desperate for spiritual consolation.

As if in answer to his prayers, events suddenly took a new turn. For some time an ambassador from Persia had been pleading for his release on behalf of the Shah and Colonel Sheil. These represen-tations from Teheran at first made little impression on the Amir. But a series of military reverses on his northern frontier, and then a further threatening note from the Shah, changed his mind. Wolff simply was not worth a trial of strength with his most powerful neighbour. Putting the best possible face on matters the Amir pretended that all along Wolff had been his honoured guest. He was now laden with presents and allowed to purchase the liberty of a few Persian slaves. An ambassador was appointed to accompany him to London and explain matters to Queen Victoria. On 3 August 1844, Wolff, with the ambassador, left Bukhara. The nightmare was over.

Nine months later, having quietly retraced his steps across Asia, he landed at Southampton. Again the crowds gathered and this time they did cheer. There too on the quayside were Lady Geor-giana, young Henry and the good Captain Grover. 'The joy,' wrote Wolff, 'cannot be expressed.' He promised never again to travel but to end his days peacefully in England. He retired to the Somerset parish of Ile Brewers and there lived and worked for another fifteen years, as much beloved for his eccentricities as for his celebrity. He never learnt to shave himself and, when reminded to change his linen everyday, he returned from a five-day tour in a pristine shirt but with four dirty ones underneath. A local reporter who attended one of his last services found him as vigorous a preacher as ever.

'As I entered the church, accents of half-broken English saluted my ear from the reading desk where stood Joseph Wolff, the great Eastern traveller, or "that sublime vagabond" as someone called him, now mumbling, now shouting his way through the first lesson. The great folio Bible and prayer book belonging to the church lay closed on the reading desk beside him as, stooping over a little manual of his own, he read the chapter. The old man began by leaning over the pulpit and, in colloquial frankness, telling us he was one who believed in the Second Coming of Christ. His vivid imagination revelled in the prospect his faith conjured up, and as the vision of Jerusalem – once again in its glory, its ancient people recalled back within its walls, filling its streets, thronging in and out its gates – arose to his mental eye, he became perfectly excited, tossed his arms aloft, waved the little black Bible in his hand, and as he cried out in transport, seemed momentarily in danger of giving vent to his feelings in a burst of song. It was with no affected ecstasy that he exclaimed, as he thought over a picture which he could not describe, "Oh indeed, it is a glorious panorama."'

6
'So Many Various Characters'
William Gifford Palgrave

To raise funds for some pious project, Father Remigius Normand S. J. was doing the rounds of Montevideo's diplomatic community. The year was 1886. Uruguay was on the verge of civil war, her ports were closed because of a smallpox scare, and times were hard. Father Remigius widened his appeal to include the embassies of non-Catholic governments; but he must have regarded the British legation as the longest shot of all. There was little love between the Uruguayans and the British; the British legation was a good three miles out of town in a most unfashionable quarter; and Her Britannic Majesty's Minister was a sick, unsociable and embittered sixty-year-old with a reputation for tight-fistedness.

His name was William Gifford Palgrave and, if his behaviour was anything to go by, he was scarcely a career diplomat. 'He does no entertaining, his dress is disreputable, and his get-up and turn-out a by-word,' wrote a correspondent of the *Nacional*. At a dinner party given by the French Minister he had presented himself 'in tweed trousers, a shooting jacket, and a bright red tie'. He was well-read – perhaps uncomfortably so – a gifted linguist, and apparently well versed in theology. But rumours about a romantic and controversial past roused little interest in the parochial atmosphere of South America's smallest republic.

Certainly Father Remigius was totally unprepared for the surprise that awaited him. Instead of a cool reception from a crusty stranger, he found himself face to face with an old colleague. Minister Palgrave, he reported, was none other than his 'quondam Jesuit brother and fellow priest'. 'The recognition was mutual but went no further,' he added. Palgrave was evidently unhappy about having his cover blown. He had nothing to hide, indeed much to boast of. But he valued his camouflages; if they had to be dismantled he preferred to do it himself. Moreover Father Remigius was not one to keep a secret. The Minister's priestly past was soon common knowledge.

Twenty-four years earlier, in very different circumstances, another ecclesiastic had been less successful in identifying the mysterious Palgrave. The Dean of Westminster, travelling as chaplain to the Prince of Wales while on a tour of the Holy Land, was encamped on the banks of the river Jordan. Over lunch in their tents, the Royal party observed a group of Arabs approaching the nearby ford. They made a picturesque sight emerging from the desert on their camels and led by a tall distinguished sheikh. Slowly they crossed the river. A messenger broke away and walked over to the tents. The sheikh, he announced, desired to speak with Dean Stanley. ''Twas a signal but somewhat trying proof of popularity,' recalled the Dean. It was also rather alarming. But curiosity soon got the better of caution. Unarmed, the little Dean walked down to the Arabs. The sheikh dismounted, advanced with great dignity and laid both hands on the Dean's shoulders. Looking steadfastly down at his guest he solemnly intoned his name.

'Arthur Penrhyn Stanley.'

The Dean peered back; he did not recognise him.

'I am Father Palgrave. My brother told me you were to be in Palestine and I heard you were going to trace the source of the Jordan.'

The two men had last met at Oxford when Palgrave was an undergraduate at Trinity College. 'What a curious meeting!' noted the Dean.

Dean Stanley, like Father Remigius Normand, would make much of this story. It lacked perhaps the poignancy of the encounter, ten years later, between that other Stanley and Dr David Livingstone. But it was not without romantic significance. Palgrave's disguise – or transformation – was the most convincing and successful in the history of nineteenth-century exploration. And April 1862, the date of the meeting, marked the beginning of his most ambitious and dangerous journey. Dean Stanley was the last European to see or hear of Palgrave for over a year.

Arabia can hardly be described as one of the most exotic arenas of exploration. In the desert all is harsh, monotonous and hostile; searing days and icy nights measured in dying camels and desiccated oases. To this austere environment orthodox Islam lends its own brand of rigid puritanism. If there was ever anything very mouth-watering in the myth of the harem, few European travellers got a taste of it. The refinements of desert hospitality, the flowery conversation, and the endless cups of coffee seem but a poor compensation.

Yet Arabia boasts a quite disproportionate number of classic travelogues, not the least of them being Palgrave's own *Personal Narrative of a Year's Journey through Central and Eastern Arabia*. The traveller to whom this austere land appealed tended to be something of a poet, responding to the mirage with visions of his own. Of deep learning and even deeper emotions he sensed both inspiration and release in the simplicity of desert life. Indeed, Burton, Doughty and Lawrence seem to have needed the baptism of burning sand as a sort of self-mortification. Whether to find, or lose, themselves, they travelled for complex psychological reasons and projected these into their travelogues. Their outsize person- alities protrude through every paragraph. Each has been described as an eccentric traveller. To relish Arabia you had to be a trifle eccentric.

In this illustrious company of tortured souls William Gifford Palgrave seems not to belong. Reading his book one is unaware of the author as anything more than an enterprising traveller and a powerful writer. Other Arabian explorers may have been, as he delicately puts it, 'too preoccupied by their own thoughts and fancies to appreciate . . . mind and manners among nations other than their own'; or else, perhaps, 'their enthusiastic imagination has thrown a prismatic colouring over the faded East'. But not Palgrave, honest Palgrave, who tells a straight story spiced with adventure, and hopes in the process to contribute something to the understanding of the country and its people. Here surely is the least eccentric of Arabists, a man with whom one might tentatively identify, certainly one to be trusted.

So at least it seemed to those who knew of him only from his *Personal Narrative*. But whether priest, sheikh, ambassador or author, there was always more to Palgrave than could conveniently be revealed. His was not so much a tortured soul as an elusive one. And his eccentricity lay not in the manifestations of an extra- ordinary personality, but in the baffling diversity of alibis under which he concealed it.

His first incarnation was as scholar and man of letters. Born into a family of dazzling talents young Gifford disappointed none of them. He was named after his godfather, William Gifford, editor of the *Quarterly Review*. At eighteen months he had learned half the alphabet and was spelling confidently at three. By five he could fill in a map of Asia. The following year he took up botany; as tutor he had a choice between his uncle, Sir William Hooker, founder of Kew Gardens, or his cousin, the great Joseph Dalton Hooker. At six his mother found him 'raving' over the Chinese alphabet, and by seven he had learnt by heart the first book of the *Aeneid* plus long chunks of Xenophon and Sallust. His first year at Charterhouse saw him warming up for the Latin prize by rendering a dozen lines of *Paradise Lost* into Latin hexameters. Divinity he enjoyed so much that he studied it in his spare time; and in mathematics he was already overtaking his elder brother – Francis Palgrave, himself no plodder and the future compiler of that standard anthology of English poetry, Palgrave's *Golden Treasury*.

Their father was another Francis Palgrave, in fact Sir Francis Palgrave, constitutional historian and founder of the Public Record Office. More significantly he was also the first Palgrave, having been born Francis Ephraim Cohen. The name Palgrave was adopted at the time of his marriage and no doubt facilitated the transformation from the newly rich Jewish household in Kentish Town to the literary circle at 50 Albemarle Street, home of the publisher John Murray; Palgrave, born Cohen, wrote Murray's *Handbook for Travellers in Northern Italy*. The Palgraves were a closely knit family bound together in love and an awareness of being newcomers. Young Gifford benefited from this intense atmosphere. But, unlike his brothers, he also cherished the less conventional and more exotic strands in the family genealogy.

Proceeding from Charterhouse to Trinity College with the inevitable scholarship he continued a brilliant student. Within two and a half years he had taken a first class degree in classics and a second in mathematics. The feat may well have been unique, but it was overshadowed by a decision for which the doting Palgrave parents could find neither antecedent nor explanation. Beloved 'Giffy', the apple of their eye, the most brilliant of their offspring, had elected to place his exceptional talents at the disposal of the Indian Army. He was already immersed in Hindustani and military strategy, and would soon disappear over the horizon bent on a profession that was as foreign and inexplicable to them as India itself. Whatever could have possessed the poor boy? Not that there was anything disreputable about soldiering in India. It was just that the Palgraves knew nothing about it and, of all people, the intellectual Gifford seemed an improbable recruit.

His academic laurels did indeed represent something of an over-kill in terms of qualifying for a cadetship in the Bombay Infantry. But he had never been a mere swot. At Oxford he rowed and played football as well as undertaking botanical rambles. He gave no reasons for his sudden about-face but it was also, doubtless, a reaction against the intellectual hothouse at home.

Committed to a life of action and exile he sailed for India in 1846. He was soon paying a heavy price. From the moment he landed in Bombay until two years later when he resigned from the army, he was never fully fit and mostly confined to bed. The irony was bitter. His sword and pistols hung on the wall, his rifle was oiled, his bull terrier pawed the door, and outside horse and groom waited in the shade. There were leopard and boar to hunt (in his new role botany had had to make way for blood sports), while up north the Sikhs were putting British India's army through its severest test. Yet the would-be man of action must toss away the breathless days bathed in sweat, babbling in delirium, and as weak as a child. In between bouts of fever he managed a little drill and worked away at his Hindustani. In 1848 he was promoted to Captain and posted to Rajkot in the remote province of Saurashtra. He was soon ill again and when the second Sikh war ended – and with it all immediate prospect of seeing active service – he resigned.

This in itself was a dramatic step; but far more unusual was the alternative career that Palgrave had mapped out for himself. In the previous year he had written home with the news that he was about to be received into the Church of Rome. His parents were distraught. Respectability counted for much in the Palgrave household. They could only hope that Giffy's little indiscretion would prove a temporary aberration brought on by the introspection of convalescence. Prayers were said, frantic letters were written to India, and the matter was hushed up. But now, as if determined to maximise the embarrassment, Gifford was resigning the army in order to join, of all people, the Jesuits.

It was not exactly treason, although many an eyebrow must have been raised in both England and India. The Society of Jesus was, after all, more than a religious order; it was an evangelising and highly controversial 'regiment' with a reputation for political guile that made the Jesuit name a synonym for devious dealing. The Jesuits had been expelled and banned in countries as Catholic as France and Spain and as recently as 1845. It was rather like joining some dubious and much detested sect. His family started to write of him in the past tense and steeled themselves for the inevitable ignominy; his fellow officers must have winced with shame; and the fathers of the College of San Giuseppe at Negapatam unashamedly gloated over their first, and undeniably distinguished, English recruit.

Palgrave himself was not insensitive to the embarrassment his decision might cause. But if he experienced any clash of loyalties it is unrecorded. With that single-mindedness which is surely the hall-mark of eccentricity, he simply followed the dictates of logic and conscience wherever they might take him. His sincerity, through numerous and bizarre incarnations, was never questioned. To each he brought utter conviction and a devastating commitment.

Four years of obscurity at the college at Negapatam were followed by two years of training and study at the Jesuit headquarters in Rome. Here he was visited by his brother Francis and his father. The latter found him 'changed and yet unchanged'.

'The child, the schoolboy, the Oxford Fellow, the soldier, the hunter, and the priest – so many various characters all distinctly visible to me and reacting upon each other most strangely. Yet all is absorbed into his calling, to which he is devoted with all his heart and soul. It is a self-imposed vow. He has counted the cost and pays it gladly.'

His knowledge of oriental languages was 'phenomenal'; he was now studying Arabic. And surprisingly, since he found even the Italian summers a trial to health, 'he yearns for Syria'.

Deep in Palgrave's complex character the Semitic chord had been struck. 'For me,' he wrote, 'what with so frequent change of abode, companions, language etc, I feel equally at home or, if you wish, equally a stranger and sojourner, as all my fathers were.' He saw himself as the wandering Jew crusading for Christianity after the fashion of St Francis Xavier. This was also the role adopted by the Christian Dervish, Joseph Wolff. But, whereas Wolff was all flamboyance and evangelism, proclaiming his unique brand of messianic prophesy from the roof-tops, Palgrave would be a model of orthodoxy and discretion, the perfect infiltrator operating behind a screen of deep learning and masterly disguise. Getting little encouragement from the Arabs, Wolff had scoured the earth in search of easier prey, especially the persecuted Jewish communities of Asia. But Palgrave was fascinated by the literature and history of Arabia. To both the scholar and the missionary this cradle of learning and religion represented the supreme challenge. He wanted nothing better than to spend his life penetrating its secrets in the Catholic cause.

In 1856 he was despatched to the Jesuit mission in the Lebanon. He was ordained in Beirut under the name of Père Michel Sohail and for four years taught and preached among the Lebanese Christians. His eloquence in Arabic led to his spearheading the search for new openings. Disguised as a sheikh he explored conversion prospects amongst the Ismailis, the Druses and the Greek Orthodox Christians of Damascus. But in 1860 an always tense situation suddenly erupted. The Druses massacred whole Christian communities, the missions were over-run, and their priests brutally tortured. Père Michel Sohail was one of the few survivors.

Later that year, still dressed as an Arab but now calling himself Father Palgrave, he turned up at the family home in Hampstead. He was on his way to Ireland to raise funds for the re-establishment of the Syrian mission. For himself, though, he already cherished an altogether more exciting ambition.

In the Lebanon, he had visited the western fringes of the Syrian desert and been seduced by the notion of exploring beyond it to the little known kingdom of Central Arabia and to the Persian Gulf. There was scant prospect of making conversions amongst a people who had never known Christianity and who regarded themselves as the guardians of Islamic orthodoxy. Nor could the Society of Jesus afford to squander its resources – and one of its most accomplished missionaries – on such a dangerous and speculative venture. But, at about this time, Palgrave came up with an ingenious way round these objections. What Arabia lacked in proselytising potential, it made up for in political potential. The existence of a power base in the uplands of Central Arabia had been common knowledge for fifty years. Napoleon had unsuccessfully sought to develop contacts with Riyadh as part of his grand design on India. More recently news had filtered out across the desert that the Wahabi princes of Riyadh had a serious rival in the princes of Jebel Shomer. Such domestic squabbles would hardly have invited European interest were it not for the fact that the Suez canal was under construction. Suddenly the existence of a formidable but virtually unknown and apparently unstable kingdom on the eastern side of the new canal became a matter of concern. And to no one was it of more interest than to the canal's principal investor, the French government.

Palgrave, now calling himself Père Cohen – at this period he was changing names more often than disguise – volunteered his services. Emperor Louis Napoleon, 'vivement intéressé', granted him an audience. He emerged with ten thousand francs and a commission to investigate and report on the Arabian political scene. It remained only for the Jesuit authorities, never averse to serving a Catholic monarch or dabbling in political intrigue, to give him their blessing. He took his final vows as a missionary, had an audience of Pope Pius IX, and in June 1861 set out for Egypt.

The scholar, soldier and priest assumed the mantle of political agent with enthusiasm. In Cairo he promoted a palace revolution aimed at nothing less than making French influence supreme in Egypt. It failed and he returned to his old haunts in the Lebanon; but he continued to file regular reports to the French Foreign Ministry. In the autumn of 1861, by way of preparation, he made a trial run across the Syrian desert to Palmyra and the Euphrates. His impersonation of a Bedouin was an unqualified success but the Jesuits insisted that in future he must travel with a fellow priest. No priest of his acquaintance measured up to his impossible standards of disguise. But there was an erstwhile pupil of his in the Lebanon, a Greek schoolteacher who had spent all his life in the Middle East, who would have little trouble in passing himself off as an Arab. Ordination appealed to the teacher and as Fr. Geraïgeri, alias Barakat-esh-Shamee, he was ready to accompany Palgrave by the spring of 1862.

From the Lebanon the two men made their way south to Gaza. Père Cohen, Michel Sohail, or Captain Palgrave now passed himself off as Seleem Abou Mahmoud-el-Eys, an Arab physician of repute from Damascus. To sustain this new persona he was armed with two or three French medical dictionaries (carefully concealed in his saddle-bags), a couple of Arabic treatises on medicine (ostentatiously displayed whenever opportunity offered), and fifty little tins of drugs, 'the wherewithal to kill or cure half the sick men of Arabia'. He wore the long loose shirt of the desert, baggy cotton trousers, red leather boots, and the Arab headscarf girt by a headband 'with some pretension to elegance'. With the addition of a capacious black cape enhancing the general air of intrigue, this was the outfit in which he had posed for a photograph to show Louis Napoleon. If one ignores the backcloth of improbably luxuriant foliage he looks most convincing. The head scarf hides the lofty brow, making the semitic nose more prominent and the eyes more fierce. A scraggy beard, already streaked with grey, hides any giveaway line of mouth or chin. A similar effect is conveyed by the profile portrait of him in Jesuit attire. No one could make himself look more conspiratorial. Yet, twenty years later, with close cropped white hair, a tidy military moustache, and in a high collar heavy with gold braid, he would be transformed into the very model of a patrician diplomat and retired Indian army officer. Disguise for Palgrave amounted to a personality change.

Barakat, the newly ordained Greek schoolteacher, passed 'in a general way' for his brother-in-law or 'appeared sometimes as a retail merchant, . . . sometimes as pupil or associate in my assumed (medical) profession'. All these roles he played with conviction. He was naturally self-effacing and utterly dependable. Palgrave would have no grounds for complaint and the man so unexpectedly ordained would one day become a Patriarch of the Greek Orthodox Church.

Together with some genuine Arab guides, this was the party that Dean Stanley met on the upper Jordan. They reached Jaffa in early May, continued south to Gaza, and then turned east into the desert. Their last port of call was Ma'an in southern Jordan.

'We found ourselves at fall of night without the eastern gate of Ma'an while the Arabs, our guides and fellow-travellers, filled their waterskins from a gushing source hard by the town walls, and adjusted the saddles and the burdens of their camels, in prepara-tion for the long journey that lay before us. It was the evening of the 16th June 1862; the largest stars were already visible in the deep blue depths of a cloudless sky, while the crescent moon, high to the west, shone as she shines in those heavens, and promised us assistance for some hours of our night march. We were soon mounted on our meagre long-necked beasts, "as if," according to the expression of an Arab poet, "we and our men were at mast-heads", and now we set our faces to the east. Behind us lay, in a mass of dark outline, the walls and castle of Ma'an, its houses and gardens, and further back in the distance, the high and barren range of the Shera'a mountains, merging into the coast plain of Hejaz. Before and around us extended a level plain, blackened over with countless pebbles of basalt and flint, except where the moonbeams gleamed white on little intervening patches of clear sand, or on yellowish streaks of withered grass, the scanty product of the winter rains and now dried into hay. Over all a deep silence, which even our Arab companions seemed fearful of breaking; when they spoke it was in a half whisper and in few words, while the noiseless tread of our camels sped stealthily but rapidly through the gloom without disturbing its stillness.'

There was already good reason for caution. Their heavily armed guides were a villainous lot even by Bedouin standards. The oases of Jauf were a good two hundred miles ahead and the intervening desert swarmed with robbers. But Palgrave was also setting the scene for his whole narrative. His plan was to cross the centre of the Arabian peninsula from the Mediterranean to the Gulf. No European had yet done this – nor had anyone entered the central Arabian capital of Riyadh. Europeans were not welcome in

Arabia. The dangers of desert travel were real enough, but the greatest danger was that of being detected as an impostor.

As Christians they ran a heavy risk. Central Arabia was the stronghold of the Wahabi Mohammedans, a reformed, puritanical and fundamentalist sect who regarded even orthodox Sunni Mohammedans as libertarians. Palgrave would conform to Islamic practice wherever possible. But it was not unreasonable for a Syrian to be a Christian and, when challenged, he would never actually deny his faith. On the other hand, as a priest, a Jesuit and a missionary he was in a very different category. Together with his civilian role of ex-British army officer turned French agent, they added up to the most dangerous set of credentials in the Arabian catalogue. Discovery on any one of these counts would herald a speedy and unpleasant death.

Palgrave was aware of this but not deterred. His faith, and in particular the Pope's special blessing, had inspired him 'with a strength and courage beyond everything human'. In a crisis this made him cool to the point of nonchalance. He actually relished such situations. The secret joy of successfully blending into the Arab scene pervades his whole narrative. The enormity of the deception, a breathless air of intrigue, and the whisper of ever-present danger are all lovingly evoked. For once in his life the elusive Palgrave was in his element.

East of Ma'an the harsh realities of desert travel posed the first challenge. Travelling eighteen hours a day during the hottest season, Palgrave and Barakat must prove themselves as tough and adaptable as their Bedouin guides. 'The days wore by like a delirious dream till we were often unconscious of the ground we travelled over and of the journey on which we were engaged.' Their food was just flour and dates; for five days they travelled without passing a well. Yet Palgrave felt the lack of sleep more than the lack of water. Mirages danced before his eyes, the landscape assumed fantastic shapes. In 'this dreary land of death' the only living things were lizards, 'with never a drop of moisture in their ugly bodies', rats, and a solitary herb; 'it was the bitter and poisonous colocynth of the desert'.

By way of encouragement he recited to himself verses from Tennyson. Lines like 'the many fail, the one succeeds' and 'trust to light on something fair' struck him as especially relevant. Tennyson was an old friend of the Palgrave family. Memories of childhood and schooldays came flooding back – a welcome distraction. Then, approaching the first oasis of Jauf, they were overtaken by the dreaded *simoon*. The sky blackened, a red-hot blast of air and sand foamed around them. Providentially they stumbled upon a solitary tent and lay there gasping as the storm passed overhead. Next day they descended into the *wadi* that led into Jauf.

The Jauf was one of the most important oasis stepping-stones in the long desert crossing from Damascus to Riyadh. Beyond the fringes of its cultivation large Bedouin encampments were strung out along the *wadi*. These were the Sherarat Bedouins, and as Palgrave's party became their guests, he embarked on a careful study of their customs and character. These sketches of Arab society are amongst his most notable achievements and nothing better illustrates the success of his disguise. He appears to have enjoyed the complete confidence of all he met and thus acquired a deeper understanding of them than almost any other European traveller. The Sherarat he could visualise neither as potential allies nor as converts. They were poor, divided and unbelievably ignorant. Yet beyond the coarse jokes and constant importuning, he found much to admire in their gauche simplicity. They were not, for instance, bloodthirsty let alone warlike.

'The Bedouin does not fight for his home, he has none; nor for his country, that is anywhere; nor for his honour, he never heard of it; nor for his religion, he owns and cares for none. His only object in war is the temporary occupation of some bit of miserable pasture-land or the use of a brackish well, perhaps a desire to get such a one's horse or camel into his possession – all objects which imply little animosity and, if not attained in a campaign, can easily be made up for in other ways, nor entail the bitterness and cruelty that attend civil or religious strife.'

The unsuspecting hospitality of the Bedouin was more than matched by the sophisticated population of the oasis itself. Palgrave and Barakat were overwhelmed with offers of accommodation and, during two weeks of recuperation, never once dined alone. Lush orchards, plentiful palm-groves, and tinkling irrigation streams made the Jauf a veritable paradise. Again Palgrave minutely detailed its configuration and society, and with Louis Napoleon in mind, emphasised its strategic importance as 'the vestibule of Arabia'. But politically it was subordinate to Jebel Shomer and to its ruler Telal ibn Rashid of Haïl. Jebel Shomer was Palgrave's next goal, the second stepping-stone on the desert road to Riyadh. In between lay the awesome Nefud, another two hundred miles of desert, this time not a pebbly plain but a choppy wind-tossed sea of the finest sand.

In the Jauf the two travellers had been pleasantly surprised by their success as merchants. Palgrave played down his medical skills and left the field clear for Barakat's retail ventures. A whole camel load of coffee beans was quickly sold off and a brisk trade in handkerchiefs, bolts of cloth, combs and beads ensued. The Jauf was a thriving entrepot but this was mid-summer and trade was at a standstill. 'For,' as Palgrave put it with feeling, 'one must be mad, or next door to it, to rush into the vast desert around during the heats of June and July.' He for one, he added, had no intention of ever making such a mistake again.

The difficulty of finding a guide or companions for the crossing of the Nefud should have forewarned him. The only people rash enough to attempt it were a party of fleeing Bedouins under the guidance of a man who closely resembled a locust – 'a half-cracked Arab, neither peasant nor Bedouin, but something anomalous between the two, hight Djedey, and a native of the outskirts of Jebel Shomer, who darkened our door in the forenoon and warned us to make our final packing and get ready for starting the same day.'

Early next morning, 'while Venus yet shone like a drop of melted silver on the slaty blue', they surmounted the encircling hills of the Jauf and launched their camels into the sands.

'Much had we heard of them from countrymen and Bedouins, so that we had made up our minds to something very terrible and very impracticable. But the reality, especially in these dog-days, proved worse than aught heard or imagined.

'We were now traversing an immense ocean of loose reddish sand, unlimited to the eye, and heaped up in enormous ridges running parallel to each other from north to south, undulation after undulation, each swell two or three hundred feet in height, with slant sides and rounded crests furrowed in every direction by the capricious gales of the desert. In the depths between the traveller finds himself, as it were, imprisoned in a suffocating sand-pit, hemmed in by burning walls on every side; while at other times, labouring up the slope, he overlooks what seems a vast sea of fire, swelling under a heavy monsoon wind, and ruffled by a cross blast into little red-hot waves. Neither shelter nor rest for eye or limb amidst torrents of light and heat poured from above on an answering glare from below.'

Their water-skins, carefully rationed and shaded from too rapid evaporation, might last them for four days. If they were to reach the first well in Jebel Shomer in that time they could afford no more than three hours a day for food and sleep. By the third day this was reduced to one hour. Their Bedouin companions were the most savage crew they had yet met. Well armed, but dressed in rags 'worthy of a scarecrow or an Irishman at a wake', they at first betrayed 'a certain insolent familiarity'. Palgrave and Barakat thought this presaged trouble and resolved to keep their distance. But, by the third day, even the Bedouin were subdued. The party had broken up into a 'sauve qui peut', each man urging on his camel with never a care for the rest.

That evening Palgrave spotted a scatter of sparrows on the sand. He remembered stories, told round the fireside, of Columbus offering thanksgiving when a bird from some unseen coast first settled in the rigging. Safety must be at hand. Barakat 'fell a-crying for very joy'. Yet 'the morning broke on us still toiling amid the sands'.

'By daylight we saw our travelling companions like black specks here and there, one far ahead on a yet vigorous dromedary, another in the rear, dismounted, and urging his fallen beast to rise by plunging a knife a good inch deep into its haunches, a third lagging in the extreme distance. Every one for himself and God for us all! – so we quickened our pace, looking anxiously before us for the hills of Djobbah which could not now be distant. At noon we came in sight of them all at once, wild and fantastic cliffs rising sheer on the margin of the sand sea.'

This was the beginning of the Nejed, the Highlands. After a day's rest at the first settlement they continued to climb the mountain ramparts of Jebel Shomer towards Haïl, the capital. They were now, at last, in Central Arabia, and Palgrave marvelled at the fertility and prosperity. In Jebel Shomer every village bespoke the industry of the people and the firm but enlightened government of their prince. All that he had heard of Telal ibn Rashid had convinced Palgrave that this man represented his best chance of furthering the interests of Paris and Rome in Arabia.

The first glimpse of Haïl, its walls and bastion towers shining in the evening sun, won his unqualified approval; 'it offered the same show of freshness and even something like irregular elegance that had before struck us in the villages . . . the whole prospect was one of thriving security, delightful to view.' In a high state of excitement the travellers entered the city and made their way to the great courtyard outside the royal palace.

It was the hour of ease and sociability. A buzz of conversation arose from the crowd of white robes and black cloaks that milled about the courtyard. At the appearance of the strangers, a slight stir was evident. Greetings were exchanged, followed by enquiries, but all of the politest nature. Then the Seyf, or Court Chamberlain, bearing a silver-plated staff, was announced – more salutations, all of the utmost formality and all answered with punctilious regard for the niceties of Arabic compliment. The Seyf beamed and Palgrave exchanged a smile of triumph with Barakat. But at that moment 'Nemesis suddenly arose to claim her due'.

In Ma'an, even in the Jauf, there had always been a danger that the missionaries might stumble on someone who would recognise them from their work in Syria and the Lebanon. But now, safely across the deserts and in the Nejed, the chances of such a disaster could be dismissed. So, at least, they had argued until that fatal moment. While happily surveying the circle of onlookers, Palgrave suddenly found himself looking straight into a face 'well known to me scarcely six months before in Damascus'. His horror may be imagined. The owner of the face, a respected merchant, 'shrewd, enterprising and active . . . and not to be easily imposed on by anyone', immediately greeted him as an old friend and boldly enquired his business in Haïl.

Palgrave stared back coldly. But the crowd must have wondered; was it stupefaction or genuine incomprehension? Before they could decide, another man stepped forward. He too claimed to have known the stranger in Damascus and clearly hinted that he must be a European. Palgrave hesitated. He suspected that this man was also telling the truth but he did not actually recognise him.

'But ere I could frame an answer or resolve what course to hold, up came a third who, by overshooting the mark, put the game into our hands. He too salaams me as an old friend and then, turning to those around, now worked up to a most extraordinary pitch of amazed curiosity, says, "And I also know him perfectly well. I have often met him at Cairo, where he lives in great wealth in a large house near the Kasr-el-Eynee. His name is Abd-es-Saleeb, he is married, and has a very beautiful daughter who rides an expensive horse."'

It was a heaven-sent fabrication. Nothing was more calculated to restore Palgrave's confidence than being accused of an impersonation he had never attempted. As a master of disguise his professional pride was touched to the quick. And as Seleem Abou Mahmoud-el-Eys, the great Damascus doctor, mistaken for some Egyptian layabout, his indignation rang true.

'Aslahek Allah – May Heaven set you right. Never did I live at

Cairo, nor have I the blessing of any horse-riding young ladies for daughters.'

The second man received an equally withering rebuke, while at the first he continued to stare with 'a killing air of inquisitive stupidity'. The crowd, loving the bit about the horse-riding ladies, was now patently on his side. The Seyf himself finally clinched matters by reprimanding the interrogators and ushering the strangers, with many apologies, into the royal palace.

Telal, prince of Jebel Shomer, more than measured up to Palgrave's expectations. A square dark figure bursting with energy, he was affable, liberal and humane, yet discriminating, courageous and steadfast. 'Amongst all rulers, whether European or Asiatic, with whose acquaintance I have ever chanced to be honoured, I know few equal in the true art of government.' Telal was clever enough to realise that there was more to his guest than met the eye. But his suspicions extended to nothing worse than that the doctor might also be buying horses for some foreign power. He made no objection to the visitors opening an out-patients' clinic and, to help establish their reputation, himself patronised it.

For six weeks Palgrave and Barakat successfully prescribed for the sick of Haïl and in the process compiled the most vivid and exhaustive dossier of the life and times of a central Arabian city. Palgrave had no brief either to negotiate with Telal or to establish a mission centre. His job was purely reconnaissance; it was more important to preserve his incognito. But he clearly saw Haïl as a launch pad for Christian endeavour and Telal as the ruler most worthy of support should Louis Napoleon decide to interfere in Arabian affairs. If nothing else transpired from his journey, he felt that the revelation of this powerful and enlightened counterweight to the authority of the Wahabi sovereign in Riyadh justified the appalling risks he was taking.

On September 8th, as part of a considerable caravan bound for Buraida, Palgrave and Barakat embarked on the penultimate leg of the journey to Riyadh. The worst of the deserts were now behind them, but the nearer they approached to Riyadh, the more charged became the political atmosphere. The Wahabis were naturally xenophobic. Their fanaticism and isolation had bred a deep distrust of outsiders. 'This is Nejed,' explained an old man to Palgrave, 'he who enters it does not come out again.' Added to this, in 1862, the Wahabis were at war, re-establishing their rule over the neighbouring province of Qasim. To avoid the hostilities Palgrave and Barakat had to make a long detour. But worse was the resultant suspicion that attached to all travellers from the outside world. It was dangerous to admit even that they came from Damascus; for might not they be spies of the Ottoman empire, and as such as unwelcome as if they were Europeans?

Palgrave now had little chance to take notes. His itinerary becomes confused and has provided subsequent travellers with ample opportunities for discrediting it. At Buraida their announced intention of proceeding to Riyadh caused still more suspicion. No one was prepared to accept the responsibility of leading two such dubious characters to the capital; for a time it looked as if they would have to abandon the plan.

On the morning of September 22nd Palgrave sat in their lodgings disconsolately reading the poems of Ibn Farid 'the favourite companion of my travels'. Barakat had gone out on a ramble round the camp of some Persian pilgrims who were heading for Mecca. This was the wrong direction for Riyadh and Palgrave thought he was wasting his time. But Barakat was an able scout. When he finally returned, grinning with triumph, he had in fact made the one contact which, in Palgrave's words, would prove 'the turning point of our whole journey'.

The man he had met was a certain Abu Isa, a Syrian who had been appointed by Riyadh as conductor of Persian pilgrims. He had just completed his spell of duty, was returning to his home at Hufhuf, and would willingly travel by Riyadh with his two fellow-Syrians. He was in high favour with the Wahabis but, better still, he was a man after Palgrave's heart.

In his published narrative Palgrave determinedly omits all mention of political and religious objectives. He says nothing about being a priest and claims that science and geography were the only reasons for his journey. But, making due allowance for such deception, it is impossible to avoid the impression that, however conscientious, Palgrave was enjoying himself immensely. He relished not only the cloak and dagger work but the whole aura of travel and adventure. Freed from the constraints of Oxford, India and Rome he was responding to people and places with a warmth that was scarcely compatible with Jesuit teaching. Long evenings spent beneath a star-filled sky, with the coffee pot going its rounds and the conversation meandering through realms of poetry and fantasy, had awakened his love of romance and a deep sense of companionship with men of alien lands and beliefs. The missionary's simple credo must have begun to seem strangely inadequate. He looked back on his own improbable achievement and was increasingly drawn towards acquaintances whose career and lifestyle mirrored his own. Such was Abu Isa, a free spirit if ever there was one. He had known more careers and identities than Palgrave. His travels embraced the East from Istanbul to India. And though intrigue and misfortune had repeatedly demolished his achievements, he remained a generous, loyal and superbly entertaining companion.

In such company the journey to Riyadh passed swiftly. It was about October 15th when they finally breasted the last rise and found themselves surveying 'the main object of our journey – the capital of Nejed and half Arabia, its very heart of hearts'.

'Before us stretched a wild open valley, and in the foreground, immediately below the pebbly slope on which we stood, lay the capital, large and square, crowned by high towers and strong walls of defence, a mass of roofs and terraces, where overtopping all frowned the huge but irregular pile of Feisal's royal castle, and hard by this rose the scarcely less conspicuous palace built and inhabited by his son Abdullah. . . . All around for full three miles over the surrounding plain waved a sea of palm trees above green fields and well-watered gardens; while the singing droning sound of the water-wheels reached us even where we had halted. . . . In all the countries that I have visited – and they are many – seldom has it been mine to survey a landscape equal to this in beauty and in historical meaning, rich and full alike to mind and eye.'

Riyadh was arguably the last of the great 'forbidden cities' to succumb to the nineteenth-century explorer. Over the centuries Mecca and Medina had been repeatedly visited. Further afield even Lhasa, Bukhara and Timbuktu had surrendered their secrets more than thirty years before. Palgrave could feel justifiably elated. But it was with reluctance that he dragged himself away from the view and descended into what he already considered 'the lion's den'.

As at Haïl, they made for the courtyard outside the royal palace. Abu Isa promptly disappeared within the massive doors, leaving Palgrave and Barakat to wait outside. Passers-by stared at them; no one approached. 'We were somewhat surprised at this unwonted absence of familiarity, not yet fully knowing its cause.' Eventually they were questioned by a smooth-tongued individual who turned out to be the Foreign Minister, and admitted to the palace. Its grim façades and labyrinthine passages reminded Palgrave of Newgate prison. Negro guards lounged against the walls, and over coffee the motley crowd of visitors appeared painfully restrained. 'The fact is that in this town, and even more of course in the palace, no one ambitious of sleeping in a whole skin can give his tongue free play.'

Meanwhile news of their arrival was having far-reaching repercussions. The blind and decrepit King Feisal, like a spider whose dusty web of intrigue had been unexpectedly shaken, was already scuttling off to the recesses of a safe country retreat. Ever fearful of assassination – the normal fate of Wahabi monarchs – he was taking no chances with the newcomers whose medical pretensions must be a euphemism for magical powers and whose Syrian origins marked them down as heretical spies.

But before deciding how to dispose of such criminals it was important to know their precise mission. Accordingly they were shown to lodgings and given to believe they were welcome visitors. They were allowed to open a surgery and to move freely within the city. Palgrave used the opportunity to compile another of his massive dossiers; it included a street-plan of Riyadh, details of its fortifications, a breakdown of the Wahabi forces, and character sketches of all the principal officials. If he met with little interference it was because the authorities knew that the information was worthless; whatever Palgrave's fate, he would never be leaving Riyadh.

Watched by the Wahabi equivalent of revolutionary guards and interrogated by a variety of honey-tongued visitors and 'patients', any mere impostor would have crumbled under the strain and anxiety. But Palgrave had now identified so closely with Seleem Abou Mahmoud-el-Eys that he lived the part. He positively enjoyed contributing his mite to Koranic scholarship in debate with the fanatical guards; or refining his mastery of Arabic idiom to strike the perfect mix of piety and politesse in fencing with his interrogators.

If anything, he erred on the side of over-confidence. In the joyless creed of the Wahabi, tobacco was as much taboo as alcohol. Yet Palgrave and Barakat continued to light their hookahs as soon as their door was closed. And when Abdullah, Feisal's eldest son, requested a pain killer for toothache Palgrave recommended tobacco 'chewed and applied to the tooth with a lighted pipe to promote its action'. It was like prescribing beef-tea to a Brahmin. 'The Wahabi said nothing, but his frown spoke much and I felt I had gone too far.' Undeterred, when asked to act as a vet at Abdullah's stables, he told the prince that in Riyadh he was in the habit of treating 'asses, not horses'. Again, 'he [Abdullah] understood the hit and was not overpleased'.

After his father, Abdullah was the most powerful figure in the kingdom. Yet Palgrave simply could not mask his detestation and contempt of him. Abdullah came to epitomise all that was most devious and detestable in the Wahabi state; a confrontation seemed inevitable. It eventually arose over a request from the prince for a supply of strychnine. Palgrave immediately suspected that if Abdullah wanted poison he must have a victim in mind and that victim must be himself. He therefore refused. The request was made again and again in ever more pressing terms. Losing patience, Palgrave told the prince, in no uncertain terms, that he knew why he wanted it. 'His face became literally black and swelled with rage; I never saw so perfect a demon before or since.'

Late that night a messenger rapped on the door of their lodgings. Palgrave was summoned to Abdullah's palace where an impromptu court of inquisition had been convened. For the first time Abdullah openly accused him of being a Christian, a spy, and a trouble-maker; the penalty was death. Palgrave admitted the first, denied the rest, and challenged Abdullah to carry out his threat. It was a clever move and, in the circumstances, so luridly evoked in his narrative, an extraordinarily brave one. Abdullah's response was to order coffee. A Negro emerged from the shadows and approached Palgrave. He bore a single cup.

'Of course the worst might be expected of so unusual and solitary a draught. But I thought it highly improbable that matters would have been so accurately prepared; besides the main cause of anger was precisely the refusal of poisons, a fact which implied that he had none by him ready for use. So I said "Bismillah", took the cup, looked very hard at Abdullah, drank it off, and then said to the slave, "Pour me out a second". This he did; I swallowed it and said "Now you may take the cup away." The desired effect was fully attained.'

He was safe for the moment. But Abdullah was now sworn to engineer his death. The only hope was escape, and with Abu Isa's invaluable assistance, this was arranged. At the hour of evening prayer on November 24th Palgrave, Barakat and Abu Isa slipped from their lodgings. They crept down the side-alleys and passages to a small unguarded gate and made for the hills. Abu Isa returned to lay a false trail and rejoined them in their desert hideout whence they made a dash east for the Gulf coast.

They arrived opposite Bahrain about Christmas 1862. Barakat then headed north, Abu Isa returned to escort more Persian pilgrims, and Palgrave sailed down the Gulf to explore Oman. He had visited Riyadh, completed the first crossing of the Arabian peninsula, and lived to tell the tale. But it was as if he could not yet face up to the decisions that now awaited him; he preferred to go on travelling. Three months later, after being twice shipwrecked and now prostrate with typhoid, he was uplifted by a steamer of the British Indian navy and conveyed to Baghdad. There he convalesced before returning to Syria, to Egypt and, eventually, in October 1863, to Rome. His narrative ends in typically mysterious style – 'Much, how much! is left untold.'

His one ambition now seems to have been to return to Syria, Egypt or Arabia as soon as possible. A host of schemes for new missionary endeavours, new political alignments, crowded his brain. But neither the French nor the Jesuits were interested. He retired to a monastery in Germany to write his book. While he wrote, the conviction grew on him that his future lay with the Arabs. He was losing patience even with Rome. He began to look elsewhere for a patron. In 1865 an announcement appeared in the British press to the effect that William Gifford Palgrave had renounced the Church of Rome and accepted an appointment as Prussia's Consul-General in Baghdad.

The new appointment, like so many over the coming years, fell through. At the last minute Palgrave changed his mind and offered his services to the British Foreign Office. The terrible King Theodore of Ethiopia had taken hostage a British consul and several missionaries. Palgrave would go and negotiate their release. In the event he got no further than Egypt. His orders were countermanded and he was posted as H.M.'s Consul at Soukhoum-Kale. It was hardly a posting designed for one of the most proficient Arabists of the day – Soukhoum-Kale was at the far end of the Black Sea under the shadow of the Caucasus. But he accepted in the hopes of something better.

Something better turned out to be first nearby Trebizond, then the island of St Thomas in the West Indies, then round the world to Manila in the Philippines. In between, during an interval of home leave, he married and was soon a devoted father. He returned from Manila with the very real prospect of at last being British Minister in Cairo. Again he was disappointed. Eastern Roumelia, a chunk of what is now Bulgaria, needed a Consul-General. And so, in 1880, did Siam.

Perhaps Palgrave failed to press his claims strongly enough. Perhaps the Foreign Office were alarmed by the ambitious nature of his approach to Middle Eastern problems. Or perhaps they feared that he still harboured some Jesuitical ambitions there.

Whatever the reason, no talent, surely, was ever so tragically wasted as Palgrave's.

By way of distraction he threw himself whole-heartedly into the affairs of each of his bizarre postings and discredited none of them. But the taint of eccentricity increasingly marred his progress. In Bangkok he responded a little too warmly to his first experience of Buddhism. When he fell ill he was invalided to Japan and there, ever vulnerable when convalescing, he fell under the spell of Shinto. While sampling its simple celebration of nature he began an epic poem, *A Vision of Life*. He was still at work on this when, with a fine sense of the absurd, the Foreign Office posted him off to Montevideo. He finished it just before he died in 1888. The poem is autobiographical, charting his spiritual and psychological quest in allegorical terms. Needless to say, it reveals little about the man who always preferred to leave 'much – how much! – untold'. But it does hint at a consistency of purpose and a sense of ultimate fulfilment which alone make sense of so perversely chequered a career.

7
'A Mistake to
Take any Notice of Him'
Dr G. W. Leitner

In the 1860s a rambling palace took shape on the outskirts of Woking in Surrey. Red-brick and neo-Elizabethan, it stood in its own rolling acres and boasted a dining hall big enough to be a hangar – which was what it became during the First World War. Designated 'The Royal Dramatic College', its original function was as 'an asylum for decaying actors and actresses'. Victorian philanthropy evidently knew no bounds; Charles Dickens himself was one of the patrons. But the running costs proved high – and perhaps the actors and actresses who would admit to being in a state of decay proved few; the Royal Dramatic College quickly fell on hard times. By 1884 the building was on the market.

It was snapped up by a schoolmaster from Lahore in India and eventually re-opened under no less improbable colours as the 'Oriental University Institute, Woking'. *Ex Oriente Lux, ex Occidente Lex* ran its motto. Where the fading stars of the music hall had relived their encores, bearded Islamic divines and genial Indian gurus now debated and studied. The great hall was turned over to a permanent exhibition of Himalayan artefacts and sculptures and, in the grounds, the dome and cupolas of a mosque appeared. It was the first mosque to be built in England and to architects more familiar with town halls than Taj Mahals it proved a nightmare. Meanwhile the Institute somehow got itself affiliated to the Punjab University and was soon handing out degrees. It might reasonably be cited as the first of the red-brick universities.

What the worthy citizens of Woking made of all this is unrecorded. No doubt there was some genteel disquiet. But mere ripples of discontent were as nothing in the tempestuous career of the Institute's founder, the distinguished and despised Dr Leitner.

Times were hard for eccentrics as Dr Leitner's experience had proved. It was the heyday of British imperialism. The exotic and loveable figures, who half a century earlier nosed their way into every corner of the globe, had gone to ground. Society was less

indulgent and the British people were taking their responsibilit
in deadly earnest. For travellers of independent mind but questionable credentials there were few opportunities and even fewer
admirers.

Their names were no longer writ large and, to find them, one
has to look further than the cross-channel ferry or the Gravesend
docks. Gottlieb Willhelm Leitner, as one might suppose, was not a
native of Woking. Born in Budapest of German parents, he had
been educated in Istanbul and then in Bursa, north of Izmir. His
date of birth is uncertain but was probably in 1839. Like many
self-publicists Leitner managed to keep his personal life very
personal. We know nothing of his parents, of why they moved
from Hungary to Turkey, or of what sort of education young
Gottlieb received. And the more is the pity; for between them
these factors produced a veritable prodigy.

According to his obituary in *The Times*, 'as a linguist he probably had no living rival'. He learnt five languages in the nursery,
spoke fifteen by the time he left school, and added one each year
thereafter. His tally at any given date was therefore about the same
as his age. With the outbreak of the Crimean war he sought his
first official appointment and was duly given a first class inter-
pretership with the British forces. This apparently carried the
honorary rank of colonel. It was a distinction of which he would
remain inordinately proud – and with good reason; at the time he
was just fifteen.

After the war he returned to Bursa and embarked on a teaching
career. To this period belongs the first of a lifetime of educational
experiments. Leitner passionately believed that 'vitality has to be
breathed into the dry bones of conjugation and declension'. It was
pointless to learn a language parrot-fashion. 'The influence of
climate and religion have to be considered as well as the character
of the people if we wish to obtain a real hold of the language of our
study.' Just as vocabularies reflected the lifestyle of a people, so
grammatical structures reflected their thought processes. His first
experiment was modest enough; he dressed up like Demosthenes
and refused to converse with his students in anything but ancient
Greek. Later he would develop these theories to the point where
language became synonymous with ethnology. As his superiors
would discover, if you invited Leitner to investigate an unknown
tongue he would produce a gazetteer of the history, homeland,
heritage and economy of those who spoke it.

Outgrowing the academic institutions of Bursa, in 1858 he
moved to London and enrolled at King's College as a post-

graduate. In turn he was appointed Assistant Lecturer and then Lecturer in Arabic, Turkish and Modern Greek. Again the prodigy was in danger of outgrowing his nest. To contain his abilities, as much as to satisfy his ambition, he began to create his own appointments; he founded the Oriental section of King's College and in 1861 was its first Professor and Dean. As if this were not enough he was also reading for the bar. By the time he was twenty-five the Professor, Dean, Master of Arts and Doctor of Letters was also a Doctor of Law.

Ex Occidente Lex; now for *Ex Oriente Lux*. In 1864 an advertisement was placed by the Government of India inviting applications for the post of Principal of Government College, Lahore. Leitner applied and, in spite of his youth and his German nationality, was appointed. No doubt his exceptional qualifications counted for much; but in the context of British India, Lahore was a special case. The capital of the Punjab province, it had been part of the British possessions for only fifteen years and still enjoyed a reputation for dynamism and experimentation. Leitner relished the idea of being free to mould its educational structure, and his colleagues in the civil administration rejoiced at the prospect of at last having a college to be proud of.

Unfortunately it soon transpired that in Leitner the Punjab authorities had got more than they bargained for. What the administration expected from the college was an inexhaustible supply of literate, English-speaking Punjabis who would fill the lower echelons of the civil service. To Leitner this was anathema. Education was not about turning out a stream of clerks but about encouraging the individual student to appreciate, and contribute to, his culture. Sanskrit and Arabic, the classical languages of Hindu and Muslim, mattered as much as English. The role of the educationalist in India was nothing less than that of fusing cultures and inspiring a new Indo-European renaissance.

With this generous interpretation of his responsibilities, the Principal of Government College set about mobilising public opinion. His early publications included three Arabic grammars, a history of Mohammedanism, an Urdu translation of *Macbeth*, journals of Sanskrit and Arabic criticism, two weekly magazines and a daily newspaper (which later became the *Civil and Military Gazette* for which Rudyard Kipling wrote). He also held regular soirées which were notable for the fact that both British and Indians were invited in a genuine effort to encourage a social and intellectual exchange between the communities. The *sahibs* viewed them with suspicion but the Indian aristocracy conceived a great admiration for the Doctor. When he asked for money they responded. For the Punjab University College the vast sum of £32,000 was raised by private subscription. This college would soon become the fully fledged Punjab University and ranks as Leitner's greatest achievement. But it was only one of nearly a hundred schools and colleges which he could – and frequently did – claim to have founded.

Had Leitner stopped there, perhaps his intolerable egotism would have been overlooked. No one could fault his dedication or deny his success; allowance had to be made for raw genius. But sadly Leitner's was a genius untempered by judgement; he never knew when to stop. If studying a language meant studying a people, then catering for their educational needs meant looking to every aspect of their welfare. Leitner appointed himself spokesman for the entire native community. He started a bank and an agricultural co-operative and even tried to reorganise the railways. Such conduct was not popular. Resentment against the mid-European intellectual who presumed to know the native mind and who dared to tell men twice his age how to do their jobs was exacerbated by his intolerable manner. Not for him the sang-froid of the patrician Englishman. He seemed incapable of conducting a conversation below the level of a debate or of completing a sentence in the same language as he began it. Whether he was right or wrong was immaterial. That unique combination of conceit, acrimony and exhibitionism which characterised the notorious 'Leitnerian outburst' invited hostility or ridicule but rarely sympathy.

In none of the spheres in which he habitually meddled would this unfortunate response have more disastrous consequences than in that of exploration. In 1865, during his first summer vacation, he visited the Himalayan valley of Kashmir and found it to be a fertile field for linguistic and antiquarian research. The Western Himalayas possess as great a diversity of races, religions and languages as any corner of the globe. At the time these had barely been charted and half the area between Tibet and Afghanistan was as yet unexplored. An added incentive was the recent discovery in the adjacent foothills of a few examples of unmistakably classical, or 'hellenistic' sculpture. One of the greatest controversies in Indian art was in the making – and no one had a better nose for controversy than the Doctor. On both scores he resolved on an early return to the mountains.

The academic year ended in April. By 7 a.m. on 1 May 1866, Leitner and a companion were on their way to Kashmir. Their route was as ambitious as the Doctor could make it. Instead of the usual two hundred miles of easy stages and gradual ascents (to a maximum of six thousand feet above sea level) he had worked out an ingenious itinerary some six hundred miles long with passes up to eighteen thousand feet. Its combination of Himalayan gradients at Tibetan altitudes was well worthy of the Leitnerian genius for taking things to extremes. Lest anyone should still be tempted to dismiss his jaunt as anything less than an epic of pioneering endeavour, he threw in the added complication of tackling the route two months before it was generally considered practicable. Mr Henry Cowie, his companion, had presumably weighed up the shortcomings of Leitner as a travelling companion; but one wonders whether either of them quite appreciated the dangers of the route.

'The paths were in many places covered by landslips. The slippery and movable planks over torrents had been carried away, the rope bridges had not yet been repaired, and accumulations of snow constantly impeded our progress. . . . On the Singun [Shingo pass into Zanskar], where we lost our way, we suffered the usual effects of continued climbing or of the rarefaction of the air, whilst nearly all our fifty coolies, men and women, became snow-blind.'

Leitner blamed the severity of the previous winter, although the conditions he mentions are by no means exceptional. Nor did snow-blind porters or spate rivers slow his progress. In little over a month the two travellers rode into Leh, the capital of Ladakh.

'In spite of our forced marches we saw a good deal that had been passed over even by so close an observer as General Cunningham [the great authority on Ladakh], whilst a variety of information was volunteered to us in acknowledgement of our friendly inter-course with the excellent Middle and South Tibetans, and in return for presents of money, or of cheap knives, scissors etc. under whose rapidly diminishing loads a number of coolies were staggering up and down the mountainsides.'

It is not clear whom he meant by 'the excellent Middle and South Tibetans', but in the Buddhist valleys of Lahul, Zanskar and Ladakh he had made a point of visiting the great monasteries. He was interested in Buddhist ritual and he was particularly inter-ested in its homeland, Tibet, whose frontier lay less than fifty miles from Leh. Since Manning's visit half a century earlier the only Europeans to reach Lhasa had been two French missionaries. Leitner thought it was high time for another attempt and was delighted when the 'abbot' of Phuktal in Zanskar offered to make two of his relatives available as hostages 'as a guarantee to our Government of his conducting an English traveller in safety to Lhasa'. In due course Leitner would publicise this offer widely. He could never quite understand why his diplomacy was not applauded and why the abbot was not taken up on his offer. Presumably the Government now realised that getting back from Lhasa was a lot more difficult than getting there. Had Leitner volunteered to go himself they might have been more enthusiastic.

Discoveries of antiquarian interest were few but he did find a piece of sculpture which appeared to represent the Buddha riding a donkey amidst waving palm fronds; was this evidence of the influence of the Jesuits who had reached Tibet in the seventeenth century? He also picked up a long cylindrical stone which proved to be an anatomically correct copy of a human phallus. After having been refused by a number of Hindu priests to whom an improved object of worship might have been deemed an acceptable present, he added it to his own collection of curiosities.

All in all the trip thus far he considered an unqualified success. 'Our experience proved that the Tibetan passes from the side of India can be crossed early in May.' It *was* a remarkable achievement but, as events would soon show, it proved nothing. Taking risks which experienced travellers regarded as unthinkable and even explorers as unacceptable, was a dangerous way of making a name for oneself.

From Leh the two travellers turned west on the last leg down to the Kashmir valley. The passes were now lower and they were on the high road between Kashmir and Tibet. The first native caravans were on the move; spring was in the air. They passed Kargil 'where there still lives the unfortunate prince whom the Maharaja of Kashmir had confined in a cage in which he could neither stand, sit nor lie down'. Then came the Dras river. A plank bridge, unrailed and covered with stones and mud, spanned the boiling snow-melt torrent. Leitner dismounted and shouted to Cowie to do the same. He was absolutely right as usual; but Cowie had evidently had enough of being ordered around.

'In spite of my warning, my companion insisted on crossing it [the bridge] on his pony, which fell into the river with its rider. I was not so fortunate as on a previous occasion; and although at one time within a yard of me, Mr H. Cowie was swept away into the middle of the torrent whence he was hurled into a waterfall and disappeared.'

Poor Mr H. Cowie. He was the brother of the Advocate-General of Bengal but other than this irrelevant detail Leitner has not a word, good or bad, to say for him. The inference must be that he was a drab and disaster-prone companion. However, if in life he had been denied prominence in Leitner's narrative, his death opened all sorts of possibilities. As luck would have it, his body was being swept down a river which flowed not south to the Indian plains but north towards a confluence with the upper Indus. Recovery of the body was therefore the perfect excuse for sending scouts into the Indus valley in Baltistan, or Little Tibet. Such a considerable addition to the range of his enquiries was more than welcome.

The last pass into Kashmir was the Zoji-la, only 11,000 feet but notorious for its freak weather conditions and attracting a far heavier snowfall than the higher but drier passes to the north and east. Leitner was now in a hurry to get down to Kashmir, he was genuinely depressed by the death of Cowie, and he must have felt that he had already been dealt his fair share of misfortune. As a result, he was 'less careful than usual'. Disaster promptly struck again. A flock of diminutive goats, acquired by Leitner in Ladakh, were found dead 'by the side of their frozen guide' on the pass. Next day 'two mules with their loads and leaders' fell through an ice-bridge and were never seen again. The goatherd, Leitner noticed, was still clutching '*in his hands*' the stockings specially provided. If only people would take his advice. He admitted that the trip had turned into 'a debacle' but he could not see why he should be held responsible. Indeed, as he tells it, the loss of the goats and the mules rankled more than that of the men.

From Kashmir he headed straight back to Lahore. Any man of average sensitivity would surely have done the same. But in Leitner's case he was not flying from the mountains to forget the whole business but to get home and proclaim his achievements. A semi-official soirée was quickly organised and to a rapt audience he recounted his version of events. He also displayed various 'ethnological acquisitions' and favoured his audience with a rendering of some Tibetan songs 'notable for their sweetness, quaintness or similarity to our own choral singing'.

Doubtless those who found Leitner most objectionable were now convinced that he was a monster. A balanced appraisal of such a controversial figure is almost impossible. Even his admirers would admit that he lacked endearing qualities. But admirers there were – and not just amongst those who had never met him. The more enlightened members of the Punjab administration, including the Lieutenant-Governor and one of the leading lights in the Asiatic Society, believed that he had a unique rapport with the native peoples and a genuine concern for their welfare. They also admired his scholarship and saw in it some political utility. Leitner wanted to return to Kashmir and extend his linguistic enquiries north and west into the mountains. This would mean exploring and exposing the state of affairs along Kashmir's sensitive and uncertain frontier – something to which the Government in Calcutta was opposed for fear of complications with its feudatory, the Kashmir Maharaja. To the provincial administration in the Punjab, however, this frontier was neither so remote nor so sacrosanct. Its unsettled condition was a threat to stability on their own frontier, and the mystery of its inhabitants, some of whom were said to be blue-eyed and fair skinned, had intrigued two generations of explorers. The Royal Geographical Society in London also regarded this area as of exceptional interest; it was one of the last slices of unexplored territory and, as the meeting place of the Himalayas, Karakorams and Hindu Kush, it represented a regrettable blank in the map of Asia.

There was no reason to suppose that Leitner would be any more successful in investigating these phenomena than previous travellers. But at least his scholarly credentials would make the attempt look fairly innocuous. His official brief, therefore, when he set off back to Kashmir only two months after 'the debacle', was to investigate the language and history of a place called Chilas. Scholars of the Asiatic Society wondered whether it had some connection with Kailas, the abode of the gods in Hindu mythology, while the politicals noted with satisfaction that it was located just across the Indus which here marked the supposed Kashmir frontier. Provided he kept his head down, it was up to Leitner what he made of the opportunity.

After a repeated assurance of the 'deep interest felt by the Government and the Asiatic Society', the Doctor bent to his task with a sigh of self-importance. He had been recommended in the first instance to solicit the co-operation of the Maharaja. This was more out of politeness than in expectation of any valued assistance; a man who put his enemies in cages was never likely to be a collaborator acceptable to the Doctor. But the Maharaja, in any case, showed no wish to collaborate and seemed, instead, set on frustrating Leitner's efforts. He refused to let him interview two Chilasi prisoners held in the capital and he arrested anyone else from beyond his frontier who attempted to communicate with the visitor.

'I began to despair that I should ever be able to accomplish the work on which I had been deputed by Government, and finally I informed His Highness the Maharaja that I was going to learn the language at Bunji on the Indus, then the extreme frontier of his country according to the treaty made with Lord Hardinge in 1846.'

The Maharaja's opposition Leitner attributed to his having ignored this treaty and frequently sent his troops across the Indus to engage the tribes beyond. Even now there were rumours of a war with Gilgit which lay even further across the Indus than Chilas. The chance of exposing a flagrant breach of treaty, and perhaps of uncovering a few atrocities, appealed strongly to the Doctor's self-righteous instincts. At Bunji, from whence a ferry over the Indus provided the only access to both Chilas and Gilgit, he would not only be well placed to study the languages but also to spy out the political situation.

The journey to Bunji involved crossing the main Himalayan chain by two formidable passes. It took him round the flank of Nanga Parbat and through some of the grandest scenery imaginable. But Leitner scarcely mentions these physical details. What contemporaries called 'the stupendous fabric of nature' interested him little. His mind was preoccupied with matters of greater moment. The Maharaja was out to stop him. Every crag might conceal a sniper and every passing traveller might be a spy. By way of guides and bodyguards he had recruited two men from Gilgit. But the night he set off they had been spirited away and replaced by two Kashmiri soldiers.

'I turned them [the Kashmiris] off when I discovered they were the men who had led an English colonel bent on reaching Gilgit a two months' dance over the hills with the sole result of bringing him back to Srinagar by a different route. I could fill a volume with an account of the hardships encountered on even the well known ground we had to traverse before reaching the little explored districts; how my followers were tampered with and my supplies cut off; how an attempt was made to draw me into a quarrel, the contemplated result of which should be my assassination. To me, whose knowledge and courteous treatment of the natives are, I may say without breach of modesty, admitted, all this would under ordinary circumstances have been a mystery.'

To the Doctor's way of thinking these difficulties only served to prove that the Maharaja had a guilty conscience about his frontier. More of a mystery, though, surrounded the Maharaja's attitude to the death of poor Cowie. Back in July one of Leitner's scouts had returned from Baltistan with the news that Cowie's corpse had at last been washed ashore. Leitner had therefore applied for permission to go and recover it, only to be told that he had been misinformed; the body had not been found and must be well on its way to the Indian Ocean. The Maharaja was quite positive about this and Leitner had let the matter rest.

Now, encamped high in the mountains en route to Bunji, he had an unexpected visit from a travelling mullah. The man drifted over to share his camp fire and during the course of the evening let slip that in Baltistan it was common knowledge that the sahib's corpse had been fished out of the river and buried in the sand. He also suggested that the Maharaja was trying to suppress the news. Why on earth the Maharaja should wish to do this he did not say. Nor does Leitner explain. Incidents and intrigues of unspecified significance are a feature of the Doctor's narrative. They give to the journey an added dimension of mystery and danger, and whatever their substance, they were real enough to him. This is not to say that he did not relish them. On the contrary, he positively looked for trouble. For, on receipt of this further news of Cowie's whereabouts, he promptly struck camp, turned about, and headed for Baltistan. The excursion would mean another two hundred miles across a desolate mountain plateau. But what was that to the chance of rescuing the restless spirit of his erstwhile companion and taking him back for a Christian burial?

'I marched day and night in order to be beforehand with the Maharaja's postal runners, passed an English officer from some Peshawar regiment who had enquired about Cowie but had been told that he had not been found, and at midnight called upon the *munshi* [secretary] of the Governor of Skardu [Baltistan], whom I ordered forthwith to produce the body. On his replying that he could not do so as it was buried four marches off, I was pacified, for my own information was thus corroborated, and I sent off a dozen men with instructions to take the whole block of earth in which the body was buried and bring it to me. The men were under the charge of Mr Cowie's bearer, Kerem Beg, who was profoundly attached to his late master, and had followed me partly in the hope of recovering his body. When it was brought in we two washed away the earth with our own hands, found the skeleton, a portion of his shawl, but no vestige of his rings, watch etc. Most singular events then happened which I must not now, if ever, relate. Suffice it to say that we found and copied a note in the

Governor's official diary in which he duly reported to the Maharaja the recovery of the body on the 2nd July 1866, whilst on the 17th August following, that potentate had denied to me the reception of any news on the subject!

'I then put the limbs into a light coffin, after wrapping them in shawl wool, linen and certain gums. An attempt was made to carry the body away, which I defeated, and against the repetition of which I guarded by keeping it under my camp bed for the remainder of my travels.'

As usual, Leitner was vindicated. He returned to the main purpose of his journey with renewed confidence and vigour. Approaching Bunji the rumours about a war between the Kashmiris and the people of Gilgit were confirmed. Hostilities had temporarily ceased but Gilgit was still being held by the Kashmiris and the fate of the prisoners on both sides was a fertile source of speculation. The tribesmen were said to use their captives as human fireworks and to round off the display by plucking out their hearts and eating them raw. Leitner turned a deaf ear to such reports. But his porters were not made of such stern stuff and absconded. Finally both his secretary and his bearer gave in notice. Their reason was that somehow news had just reached them that both their mothers had been taken dangerously ill. Quick as a flash the 'authority on the native mind' saw through this little subterfuge. 'I gave them a lesson and dismissed them as faithless to their salt, and went on alone when, to my great pleasure, they turned up again a mile or two further on, and implored me to take them back into my service.'

A descent of six thousand feet finally brought them down from the chill air of the mountains to the sweltering desert of the Indus valley. At only three thousand feet above sea level the temperature here in August would have been about a hundred degrees. Sand and rock shimmered in the hard white light and the surrounding heights served only to wall in the heat. Behind the travellers a cloud of dust hung in the heavy air like a vapour trail. A more dramatic change of temperature is not to be found. Yet Leitner was as oblivious of the climate as he was of the landscape. The scattering of low mud huts that was Bunji loomed ahead. He appropriated the first shed he came to and was delighted to find its owner speaking the language he had come so far to study.

Whether the man was actually from Chilas is not clear. Leitner had now discovered that Chilasi was only one of a host of tongues spoken by the people across the river. In the Hindu Kush it appeared that each valley was a separate political entity with its own customs and language. Leitner therefore widened his field of enquiry to include all these peoples and, by way of justification, lumped them all together under the title of 'Dards'. The whole Himalayan region of what is now Pakistan therefore became 'Dardistan'. He did not quite invent these terms. Classical geographers had mentioned a Himalayan people called the *Daradae* and more recent travellers had revived the term to differentiate the Caucasian peoples of the Western Himalayas from their Indian (Kashmiri) and Mongol (Tibetan) neighbours. But Leitner was certainly the first to popularise the word and the first to give any serious study to the Dard languages.

Even to a linguist 'with no living rival' these unknown tongues presented a formidable challenge. For one thing they had no script. Leitner's method was first to build up a basic vocabulary by pointing at things. In this way he quickly learnt several different Dard words for finger and a number of other expressions later found to be threats and terms of abuse. Eventually, though, the Dards got the hang of the game and a vocabulary did begin to emerge. By making the appropriate gestures he also learnt 'expressions for the simplest bodily wants'. The grammar presented the greatest problem. 'It was more difficult to follow the imperative form in the commands given by my companions and to trace an affirmative or the present or future indicative in their replies.' A peculiar feature of all these languages was that each verb had a different form depending not only on tense, causality, habit, potentiality etc. but also on the gender of the person speaking and the proximity of the object he was speaking about. The resultant variety of inflexions exceeded anything Leitner had ever encountered; the root of the verb became so submerged in them as to be indistinguishable.

'Often when almost sure of a form I have discovered that the person addressed did not understand my question or had made use in reply of an idiom or an evasion. However, by asking the same question of several people, by making them ask each other, and by carefully noting their replies, I gradually reached that approximative certainty which alone is attainable in so complicated a matter. When it is considered that I was finally able to put down songs, legends and fables; that the dialogues on every subject that one discusses with a Dard show idiomatic deviations in practice; that these dialogues, vocabularies and songs extend not to one but to four languages and four dialects; it must be admitted that I have rendered some service to linguistic science.'

At Bunji he had progressed no further than the finger-pointing stage, when the governor of the place got wind of his arrival. Kashmiri soldiers promptly surrounded him and proceeded to turn away his new Dard friends. To the Doctor this was the last straw. He tried unsuccessfully to see the governor, and then stormed down to the river bank. Conveniently the ferry was to hand. He commandeered it and, with the Kashmiris apparently impotent in the face of such impulsive behaviour, he crossed the river. In doing so he became only the second European ever to have entered Dardistan; and since his predecessor had left no record of his journey, his would be the first account of the trans-Indus peoples.

The other bank, and indeed all the ground as far as Gilgit, was still in the hands of the invading Kashmiris. Seeing the sahib being confidently paddled across the swirling waters in their only boat, the troops on the other side naturally assumed that his visit had been authorised. Leitner was received with 'almost royal honours'. He quickly pressed on into the arid hills before word of his having broken bounds could overtake him.

'I went on through burnt out villages, and along paths here and there disfigured by hanging skeletons of people said to have been insurgents against the Maharaja's authority, but declared by the natives to be peaceful peasants hanged in order to support false rumours of victories. I carried my cork bed, light as a feather, myself and, like my secretary and bearer, was armed with two revolvers whilst my pockets contained pots of Liebig's Extract.'

A cork bed and pots of Bovril – it was not quite what the Victorian public expected of its intrepid explorers. But then this was no ordinary foray into *terra incognita*. Leitner was on the run and probably already regretting his impetuosity. To assess the situation, and to get out of the sun, he and his followers crawled into a little stone hut beside the road. At that moment a breathless Kashmiri post-runner approached and hurled a letter through the open door. The hut was evidently a staging post and, by the sort of coincidence that could only happen to Leitner, the letter just happened to be that to the Governor of Gilgit warning of the sahib's approach and authorising his arrest. The letter went no further. Leitner regarded the incident as a happy omen and resolved to press on for Gilgit.

They crossed the ridge between the Indus and Gilgit rivers and bivouacked for the night amongst fallen boulders. In the dark an exchange of gunfire roused the Doctor from his cork bed. An armed gang under the command of a Dard – 'whose appearance, yellow moustache and cat-like eyes, reminded me of an acquaintance during the Russian war of 1855' – had tried to rush them but had been repulsed by the two servants. Leitner was relieved to learn that the man was in the pay of the Kashmiris; it would have been galling to meet with hostility from the people whose cause he had come to espouse.

'Next morning I trod on a stone trap, the effect of which is to loosen the mountainside and to hurl one into the abyss below – a stratagem often successfully adopted by the Dards against the invading Kashmir troops. I was saved by accidentally falling backwards.'

Luck was still on his side. Further on, a couple of straying ponies awaited their convenience. Leitner and his secretary mounted and rode the few remaining miles to the Gilgit fort. The gaunt and timbered building they found poorly guarded and currently being used as a hospital. Sick and disabled soldiery filled the courtyards; 'the stench was abominable'. Outraged by the general air of neglect Leitner called for the commandant who arrived 'bleary-eyed from an opium siesta'.

'Although I was dressed as a Bokhariot mullah and armed with a numerously signed certificate of sanctity, I neglected the first and only opportunity I ever had of possibly benefiting by a disguise, for I at once stated that I was a European and that I ordered him immediately to clean out the place.'

Unfortunately Leitner also neglected to explain how it was that yesterday's pistol-toting sahib with his pockets full of Bovril had become today's well-accredited mullah from Bukhara. An engraving in one of his books shows him, chubby and heavily bearded, in the turban and robes of his disguise. But again the caption offers no explanation. Is it to be credited that the outfit was part of his normal travelling wardrobe? Or was there a real Bukhara mullah stranded somewhere between Bunji and Gilgit in his underwear?

The commandant of the fort complained that he had received no instructions about accommodating either a mullah or a sahib – 'of which,' noted Leitner in parenthesis, 'I knew the reason.' However, he supposed he should offer him protection and yes, he would clean up the fort. Leitner spent the night in the fort's mosque but found the stench of partially buried bodies too much. Next day he moved out to a ruined village nearby. The Dards whom he was so anxious to meet were still conspicuous by their absence and likely to remain so for as long as he accepted Kashmiri protection. But here in the open countryside he was on neutral ground. With a naivety wondrous to behold he decided to invite them to a soirée. A drum was borrowed from the fort and all day his bearer marched up and down the devastated valley banging and shouting the good news 'to what appeared to be the desert air'. But high on the rocky hillsides and deep in the overgrown orchards Dards in ambush observed matters and considered. The sight of cooking and the smell of roasting sheep finally decided them. Under cover of darkness groups of heavily armed warriors gathered in the shadows round Leitner's camp. Amazingly, it had worked. 'About a hundred and fifty men came, whom I entertained and who danced.'

It was the most exciting and decisive evening of his life. The Dards – men from Chilas and Gilgit, from Hunza and Yasin in the north, and from Chitral on the Afghan border in the west – stuffed themselves with mutton and apricots, then rose singly and in set groups to sing the haunting songs and dance the slow rhythmic dances of the high Hindu Kush. Teeth and weapons glinted in the firelight. The music of fife and drum rose on the still air and Leitner, pistol in one hand and pen in the other, smiled benignly on as he worked away at his vocabularies. To him the wild piratical-looking figures were true freedom-fighters. He believed their racial origins to be of the purest Aryan type and their culture, as represented in their languages, to be equally ancient. But both were now endangered by the savage and illegal oppression of a British feudatory. How could he do other than repay the trust they were showing him by representing their plight to the outside world?

Next day, 'fearing that another attempt on my life might be successful' and 'anxious to give no fixed locality or time for the assassination', he made a dash back to Bunji. He had been in Dardistan for just three days. Those who wished to discredit him would make much of the fact that his pontifications were based on an acquaintance of less than seventy-two hours. But the Doctor had ready his answer. He did not pretend to be an authority on the geography, just the people. And to accomplish that, his home in Lahore would henceforth become a permanent refuge for Dards. Its first few inmates now accompanied him back across the Indus after a cut-throat's farewell to their families.

'One of them, otherwise a nice fellow, I stopped in the attempt of cutting off the head of his mother. The good son merely wished to prevent her from dying of grief in consequence of his departure.'

The return journey to Srinagar, the Kashmir capital, was as usual packed with incident. At the fort of Astor he was 'involved in difficulties' while trying to ascertain the fate of some Dard women from Yasin ('as fair as any English woman') whom the Kashmiris had captured after massacring all their menfolk; as Leitner feared, they were destined for sale to the highest bidder. At Astor he also reclaimed the coffin containing Cowie's gruesome remains; surprisingly it had not been tampered with. Two marches further on he was ambushed by some Kashmiri snipers and managed to teach them 'a lesson they will never forget'. Next he encountered a man who claimed to be a teacher from the Punjab but who was being dragged off to Gilgit because the Kashmiris thought he was a doctor. Leitner could hardly resist coming to the rescue of a fellow schoolmaster 'and a British subject to boot'. 'I got into some trouble on that man's account.'

In Srinagar the Maharaja publicly received him with honour but was unavailable when he tried to protest about affairs on the frontier and secretly offered a hefty bribe for the Doctor's silence. Leitner declined it with lofty propriety. He then blotted his copybook by contriving a sordid row with the British Resident in Kashmir. The Resident wanted to relieve him of Cowie's coffin and bury it forthwith. Leitner objected. There was no minister in the valley and he had not brought it with him this far to have it again interred on foreign soil without the benefit of clergy. The Resident protested that, like the captain at sea, he was empowered to do the honours. Leitner was unmoved. The coffin, like the clutch of wide-eyed Dards, numerous artefacts, weapons, copies of inscriptions and a Tibetan mastiff named Chang, were all part of his haul of curiosities. He would part with nothing before he reached journey's end.

With only a few days' leave remaining he hastened away 'carrying Cowie's body myself when I could not immediately obtain coolies'. By marching round the clock he covered the last two hundred miles in four days and on the evening of October 20th presented himself at the residence of the lieutenant-governor of the Punjab. 'I was received with great kindness, in spite of my dilapidated appearance and the presence of a small party in evening dress.' Official acknowledgement of his 'great exertions' followed in due course. Cowie's remains were at last laid to rest, the Dards were installed in the compound of his bungalow, and Leitner was given another three months' vacation to elicit the remaining secrets of the Dard languages and to embody them in a book. It was nothing like long enough, and over the next few years he would repeatedly plead for more time. However 'it was decidedly more pleasant to write down what they said while seated at a table, even under a punkah, than to stand or walk with one hand ready for the revolver and the pencil in another, or, worse still, to sit half blinded by the camp smoke and try to put down songs, whilst anticipating a surprise or the treachery of old or new friends.'

In 1867, as proof of their interest in his enquiries, the Government obtained from the Maharaja of Kashmir some more Dard prisoners to add to his collection. They included two Chilasis and four Kafirs, representatives of the most primitive of all the Hindu Kush tribes. Leitner himself recruited men from Baltistan and from Yarkand in what is now Chinese Sinkiang. Others – poets, musicians and scholars from all over Central Asia – dropped in whenever their travels took them to Lahore. The Doctor's compound became not just a centre of Dardic studies but an ethnic zoo. Whilst other sahibs proudly posed for the camera amidst skins, horns and antlers, Leitner ranged himself no less proudly amongst his assorted Dards. He even paraded them in London society, taking home a Yarkandi in 1868, a Kafir in 1873 and a native of Hunza in 1887; each was the first of his race ever to be seen in England.

Leitner's critics bemoaned such publicity-seeking antics, but the Doctor had his reasons. For one thing the publication of his linguistic studies had not won the applause they deserved. The first Dard vocabularies and dialogues appeared in the late 1860s under the title *Results of a Tour in Dardistan*. Only one hundred copies were printed and very few of these were sold.

'Unfortunately I believed at first that scholars had only to see the results in order to judge of their value by comparison and inner evidence. Instead of this, it was asked how it was possible that one man could have collected so much within so short a time – as if I could possibly be held responsible for the slowness of comprehension of others or their inability correctly to catch a sound.'

It was also asked why he had published no account of the journey. At first he took exception to this too, 'as if I had worked to amuse the general reader, and not to instruct the scholar'. Besides, did people not realise that he had been engaged on an official mission and was therefore not at liberty to publish what he pleased? Later, forgetting these objections and presumably stirred into action by the indifference shown to his first publication, he did produce a

Rough Outline of a Tour and this, like everything else he wrote about the Dards, was reprinted in his subsequent books about Dardistan. Just seven pages long it is scarcely a classic of travel. Again it was ignored, and not just by the general reader but even by subsequent visitors to the region.

Anyone less convinced of his own genius would surely have despaired of recognition. The authorities – and that meant the British – seemed determined to under-rate everything he did. Whether on the subject of education, exploration, scholarship or politics, he was met with the same tolerant smiles and the same evasive answers. Was it because he did not belong, was not a member of the Anglo-Indian establishment, not even a British subject? In 1872 he exchanged jobs with the Punjab's Inspector of Schools and spent a year touring the foothills. He discovered yet another family of Himalayan languages and collected a vast quantity of Indo-Hellenistic (or nowadays 'Gandhara') sculptures. These, together with one of the Kafirs, he took to Europe in 1873.

The main purpose of his European visit seems to have been to win that recognition which eluded him in India. He therefore took part in the 1873 Universal Exhibition held in Vienna and, in competition with several national Ministries of Education, succeeded in winning a coveted diploma for the promotion of education. This was a substantial achievement and a well-deserved one. His exhibit, besides displaying all his publications and a list of his educational foundations, included 1000 ancient coins, 184 sculptures, 3200 Himalayan butterflies and beetles (presumably borrowed, since there is no record of his being an entomologist), 25 rare manuscripts, 197 'industrial articles' etc. etc. And the whole thing was presented to the international audience in fifteen different languages.

Recognition of a sort quickly followed. He was made a Knight of the Order of the Iron Crown of Austria and an Honorary Member of the Hungarian Academy of Sciences, the French School of Oriental Languages and the German Hochstift. Even in England he was invited to address several of the learned societies and acquired at least one sincere admirer. This was J. H. Stocqueler, editor of a magazine called *The Oriental*. He immediately embarked on a serialised biography of the Doctor. 'A very extraordinary man from every point of view', concluded Stocqueler after thirty pages of fulsome compliments.

The only revelation contained in *The Oriental* was that in 1874 Leitner visited Iceland – 'where he succeeded in deciphering an inscription in Hruna' – and Greenland where he discovered a glacier of a hundred miles in length. How much longer he spent away from India is not known, but he was certainly back at his post in Lahore by the early 1880s.

There must have been another spell of home leave in 1884, for it was then that he purchased the Royal Dramatic College, Woking, as the future home of the Oriental University Institute; the funds were provided by his ever loyal Indian admirers. It was probably also on this visit that he at last became a naturalised British subject. Both decisions reflected his growing disillusionment with the educational system in India, coupled with an awareness that the Dards would get a more sympathetic hearing from academics and philanthropists in Europe than from anyone in India.

Ironically the Government of India chose this moment to make a belated recognition of his linguistic researches. His last spell of duty was spent not at Government College, Lahore, but 'on Special Duty with the Indian Foreign Department' with instructions to compile a vocabulary and grammar for the language of Hunza and the neighbouring state of Nagar. Leitner was not permitted to visit either place but he again interrogated his two Hunza retainers and scoured Kashmir for others. Their language, Burishaski, was the most difficult and intriguing of all the Dard tongues. Its only affinity seemed to be with Hungarian or possibly Basque and in its use of a single consonant to express a basic idea he thought he detected 'the cradle of human thought as expressed in language'. Carried away by his own philological enthusiasm he lobbied the Foreign Department to extend his term of duty and to consider further investigations into all the languages of the Hindu Kush, indeed of Central Asia. The advance of Russian influence north of the mountains had suddenly endowed the region with immense strategic importance. If the support of the Dards and their neighbours was to be secured, what could be more valuable than a knowledge of their languages and an understanding of their customs?

The Indian Government was now well aware of the vulnerability of the mountain frontier and needed no lecturing from Leitner. In 1886 a large mission was in the process of exploring the country and concluding treaties with the Dard tribes. On its recommendation Gilgit would become a British base and in 1889 a British Agent took up residence there. In the same year Leitner's *Hunza-Nagar Handbook* appeared. 'It reminds us of the Talmud,' wrote a reviewer in *The Times*; he found its variety of information truly wonderful. The Government of India was less impressed. It quibbled about the time and expense involved and there is no evidence that any of its officers in Dardistan ever used the book. On the open market only one copy had been sold two years after publication.

Meanwhile Leitner had retired to Woking. The Oriental University Institute was to be his showpiece, a permanent home for his assorted collections and a working model of how the educational systems of East and West could be fused together. The sculptures, the butterflies, and even the occasional Dard, went on display, the students took up residence, and the mosque was begun. The Institute was also, of course, a publishing house and for its first publication Leitner chose a new edition of the *Hunza-Nagar Handbook*. It bore the imprint of the Institute and it certainly appeared to be a new edition. But the Government of India was not so sure. Enquiries were made and it transpired that a hundred copies of the original edition were indeed missing; the author had apparently appropriated them 'as an honorarium'. The 'new' edition had, it was true, some extra appendices – so many in fact that they were issued as a separate volume. But even these were not exactly new since every one of them was a reprint from an earlier article.

No action was taken, probably because the authorities were more concerned by the Institute's new periodical, the *Asiatic Quarterly Review*. This did contain new material and very little of it was of a welcome nature. In the early 1890s the Indian Government – or rather, its officers in Gilgit – embarked on a series of repressive campaigns aimed at bringing the still recalcitrant Dard tribes firmly to heel. Leitner opposed this policy with vigour and venom. At public meetings, in the national press and, at great length, in the *Asiatic Quarterly Review*, he defended the Dards and savaged their oppressors. It had been bad enough when he caught the Maharaja of Kashmir interfering in Dardistan. But this imperial bullying of a unique, inoffensive and fiercely independent people was a crime against humanity.

As usual, the Doctor overflowed with self-righteous indignation and could not resist the opportunity to parade his exceptional knowledge of the area. It was this candour which so upset the authorities. In correcting the invariably misinformed statements put out by the Government he let slip information which could be considered as of value to the Russians. According to the then Viceroy, this was 'clearly done for disloyal motives'. The Secretary of State cautioned leniency. The *Asiatic Quarterly Review* was 'a struggling journal' and Leitner's contributions were invariably 'egotistic and worthless'; to take issue with him would only give him the satisfaction of further publicity. The Hon. George Curzon, future Marquess and Viceroy who was himself just off to Dardistan, seems to have decided the matter with a typically curt and damning note.

'I know Dr Leitner and his Review. The latter carries little weight, the former none. It would be a mistake to take any notice of him.'

Compiling his dossiers on the Dards, Leitner had been much taken by their legends and cautionary tales. One such, distilled into an aphorism, he had translated as 'A sparrow who tried to kick a mountain himself fell over'. It was an apt allegory of his own situation. The more he protested the innocence of the Dards and the danger of coercing them, the less he was heeded. He ranted against the careerist subalterns ever spoiling for a new campaign and another medal. He ridiculed the political officers whose ignorance was rivalled only by their arrogance. He even offered to visit Dardistan himself and use his good offices to bring about a peaceful solution. But it made not a jot of difference. In 1891 Chilas was invaded, in 1892 Hunza and Nagar and in 1892 and 1895 Chitral. By 1896 it was all over. Dardistan was 'pacified', the Dards tamed and tainted, and Leitner conceded that his crusade had failed.

'All in vain. No one perhaps has struggled more on behalf of the Dards and Kafirs than myself during thirty years, but the cause is lost and now their only chance of survival is a complete and loyal acquiescence in the new order of things.'

Three years later Leitner died of pneumonia. The Oriental University Institute died with him and the building was sold; only the mosque remained as a monument to his memory.

Bibliography

Chapter 1
Thicknesse, Philip, *A Year's Journey through France and Part of Spain*, Dublin 1777; *Memoirs and Anecdotes*, 1788
Adair, J. M., *Medical Cautions*, 1787
Gosse, Philip, *Dr Viper, The Querulous Life of Philip Thicknesse*, 1942

Chapter 2
Markham, C. R. (ed.), *Narrative of the Mission of George Bogle to Tibet and of the Journey of Thomas Manning to Lhasa*, 1876
Anderson, G. A. (ed.), *Letters of Thomas Manning to Charles Lamb*, 1925
Lucas, E. V. (ed.), *Letters of Charles Lamb*, 1935
Woodcock, George, *Into Tibet, The Early British Explorers*, 1971

Chapter 3
Holman, James, *Narrative of a Journey through France, Italy etc.*, 1822; *Travels through Russia, Siberia etc.*, 1825; *A Voyage round the World*, 1834
Jerdan, W. M., *Men I have Known*, 1866
Cochrane, J. D., *Pedestrian Journey through Russia and Tartary to Kamtchatka etc.*, 1825

Chapter 4
Waterton, Charles, *Wanderings in South America*, 1823; *Wanderings in South America* (ed. L. Harrison Matthews), 1973; *Essays on Natural History*, 1838–57
Waterton, Charles, *Letters* (ed. R. A. Irwin), 1955
Hobson, R., *Charles Waterton, His Home, Habits and Handiwork*, 1866
Aldington, R., *The Strange Life of Charles Waterton*, 1949

Chapter 5
Wolff, Joseph, *Researches and Missionary Labours etc.*, 1835; *Travels and Adventures*, 1860; *A Mission to Bukhara* (ed. Guy Wint), 1969
Palmer, H., *Joseph Wolff*, 1935

MacLean, Fitzroy, *A Person from England and Other Travellers*, 1958

Keay, John, *When Men and Mountains Meet*, 1977

Chapter 6

Palgrave, W. G., *Personal Narrative of a Year's Journey through Central and Eastern Arabia*, 1868

Palgrave, W. G., *A Vision of Life*, 1891

Allen, Mea, *Palgrave of Arabia*, 1972

Freeth, Z., and Winstone, H. V. F., *Explorers of Arabia*, 1978

Chapter 7

Leitner, G. W., *Results of a Tour in Dardistan*, Lahore 1877; *The Languages and Races of Dardistan*, Lahore 1889; *The Hunza-Nagyr Handbook*, Woking 1893; *Dardistan in 1866, 1886 and 1893*, Woking 1893

Stocqueler, J. H., *The Life and Labours of Dr G. W. Leitner*, Brighton 1872

Keay, John, *The Gilgit Game*, 1979.